T0128925

THE CRADLE OF
TEXAS
ROAD

A Model of Cultural Integration for the Nation

*Robin Navarro Montgomery, PhD,
and Joy Montgomery*

iUniverse, Inc.
Bloomington

The Cradle of Texas Road
A Model of Cultural Integration for the Nation

Cover design by Theresa Thornhill and Joe Kolb

iUniverse books may be ordered through booksellers or by contacting:

iUniverse
1663 Liberty Drive
Bloomington, IN 47403
www.iuniverse.com
1-800-Authors (1-800-288-4677)

ISBN: 978-1-4759-8005-9 (sc)
ISBN: 978-1-4759-8006-6 (hc)
ISBN: 978-1-4759-8007-3 (e)

Library of Congress Control Number: 2013904245

Printed in the United States of America

iUniverse rev. date: 3/18/2013

About the Authors

ROBIN NAVARRO MONTGOMERY

Robin Montgomery is a native of Conroe, Texas and holds a PhD from the University of Oklahoma. His professional background includes a career as university professor at Southwestern Oklahoma State University and Oxford Graduate School, along with four years as professor of international relations for a graduate program in Europe for US military officers. Among his organizational experiences, he is a member of the International Oxford Society of Scholars. He has published extensively in both political science and local history, articles, books and newspaper columns. His previous books on local history include: The History of Montgomery County, Texas (Two editions); Cut'n Shoot, Texas; Tortured Destiny: Lament of a Shaman Princess (historical novel); Historic Montgomery County: An Illustrated History; Indians and Pioneers of Original Montgomery County; March to Destiny: Cultural Legacy of Stephen F. Austin's Original Colony; with Joy Montgomery, Navasota: Images of America and, with Roy Harris, Roy Harris of Cut and Shoot: Backwoods Battler.

JOY RENEE MONTGOMERY

Joy Montgomery holds an M.A. degree in English and History from Sam Houston State University. Her B.A. degree is in German. While studying in Germany, she achieved officially sanctioned fluency in that language. Her professional career includes teaching positions in Germany, South Korea and Kyrgyzstan, the latter while a member of the US Peace Corps. Also, she has worked with the Department of Housing and Urban Development in Washington, D.C. She is currently the executive director of Texas Center for Regional Studies. Her publications include Navasota: Images of America, with Dr. Robin Montgomery.

Contents

PREFACE

Purpose of the Study

Our nation is facing a crisis of cultural polarization. Without a common set of values or traditions to monitor the communication process, whole groups of people are isolated from each other. Clear understanding of the words or expressions of people is rendered difficult when there is no common perspective. As a measure to enhance cultural integration as an avenue to prosperity, this study explores the use of history as a common framework or reference point. Accordingly, within these pages is employed an interpretation of history featuring a theme common to a particular region, in this case the region just north of Houston, Texas.

A framework for portraying historical commonality on a regional level, it is submitted, can serve as a model upon which to reflect in the search for a national consensus. The model provides a foundational framework within which to showcase different conditions, events and innovative personalities, both present and past, distinctive to the various communities of the area under study. The common historical focus dilutes tendencies toward polarization through generating a sense of regional pride. It is to be hoped that the regional pride will spill over into activities in multiple arenas, social and economic, serving to enhance communication both between and within the communities of the region.

Birth of the Vision

On 5 May 2012, The *Texas Center for Regional Studies* orchestrated a *Texas Legacy Fest* in Navasota. The fest centered on a rededication of a statue of René Robert Cavelier Sieur de la Salle.

The idea for the rededication ceremony stemmed from reflection on the contribution of La Salle to the greater history of Texas. These reflections revealed that La Salle's presence north of the Rio Grande was the fundamental agent conditioning the Spanish to seek to colonize their lands north of that great river. It was upon finding La Salle's by then abandoned Fort St. Louis off Matagorda Bay in 1689 that the very next year the Spanish established a presence east of the Trinity. It was during that expedition that they named the area Texas.

Given this sequence of events, La Salle's name may legitimately be associated with the word "cradle" in the sense of giving birth to an event. Further reflection along these lines led to the conclusion that other sites along a network of roads near Navasota, where La Salle met his demise, could also be associated with the label of cradle; hence the basis for the vision of a Cradle of Texas Road.

(*See supplement one for a feature article on La Salle's Texas Legacy*)

Marriage of Two Visions

This book represents the marriage of the vision of a Cradle of Texas Road to that of a second *Texas Legacy Fest*, this one slated for Conroe, Texas on 12-13 April 2013. Celebrated will be the 200th anniversary of the First Republic of Texas. This *Texas Legacy Fest* provides a capstone for the saga of the Cradle Road for while the first republic took root in San Antonio, it was declared initially near present Madisonville, at the apex of the Cradle Road.

The first republic marked the birth of something unique in the annals of the Western Hemisphere, the joining of representatives of multiple cultures to form a new political system. Anglos, Native Americans, Mexicans and African-Americans joined forces as one to create the first, or Green Flag Republic, giving it the distinction of being the Cradle of Democracy in Texas. Like the 1st Republic of Texas, the Cradle of Texas Road is centered on the theme of bringing people together for a common purpose, building a foundation for cultural integration.

(*See supplement two for a feature article on the Green Flag Republic*)

Support Personnel

Providing the initial momentum and support behind this book was Theresa Thornhill. Hers was the pivotal vision of a mural depicting the historical and symbolic dimensions of the Cradle of Texas Road. The vision of the mural reflects her tenure as president of the Conroe Art League and CEO of her company, Digital Accents. With Theresa Thornhill, co-artist, Joe Kolb, inspired the cover for the book.

Other people indispensable to the study were Maria Jordan, Director of the Texas Latino Leadership Roundtable; Rita Wiltz, Head of "Books on Wheels," Dr. Leslie Holtkamp, Chief of School

Choice Initiatives Willis ISD, Jessica Paschal, Tourism and Events Coordinator for the Conroe Convention and Visitors Bureau; Larry Foerster, Chair of the Montgomery County Historical Commission; Dr. Ahia Shabaz, President of the Pan American Roundtable and Alejandra Tapia, Director of Chikawa Aztec Dance and Traditions. Also providing crucial support were Carl Smith of the Texas Center for Regional Studies and Evelyn Barden, Beverly Montgomery and Luke Austin Mitchell.

PART I.

Cradle of Texas Road:

Sites and Side-Trips

INTRODUCTION

Washington Municipality, Birth and Impact

The Cradle of Texas Road is an intersecting series of highways enclosing a cultural enclave of communities and sites distinctive in Texas history. We begin our journey with a review of the common historical nexus out of which these communities and sites emerged.

In 1835, the Mexican government created Washington Municipality, a political unit covering all or part of nine present Texas Counties on either side of the Brazos River. Upon declaring their independence from Mexico at Washington on the Brazos on 2 March 1836, on 17 March the Texans labeled the 23 Mexican Municipalities as of that date as counties. Accordingly, Washington Municipality became Washington County. On 14 December 1837, Washington County east of the Brazos became known as Montgomery County eventually extending from the Brazos to the Trinity Rivers and from Spring Creek to the Old San Antonio Road. This vast area included later Grimes, Walker, Montgomery and part of Madison, San Jacinto and Waller Counties. Framed within this region and nearby Washington-on-the-Brazos is the Cradle of Texas Road. (For details of the organization of Washington Municipality and the birth of the counties that were its offspring see Robin Montgomery, *March to Destiny*, a basic source for this chapter).

Overview: Cradle Road

Beginning at Madisonville, our road traverses highway 90 south to Navasota where it links to highway 105 and on westward to Washington-on-the-Brazos. Extending west to east from Washington to Conroe and beyond to Cut and Shoot and the Latino community of Deerwood, it then, upon retracing its path to Conroe, turns north to follow Interstate 45 through Huntsville and back to Madisonville. Along the way, featured are selected communities and historical sites. Each of these, it will be shown, harbors a significant event or personality which accords to the theme of birth in terms of initiating some unique contribution to Texas history and culture. It is in this sense that the route may be referenced as the *Cradle of Texas Road*.

After a little background on events giving rise to Washington Municipality and the political entities that are its offspring, we will visit the respective spots along the road, as well as take some exciting side trips along the way.

In the Beginning: Rise of Austin Municipality

Our Cradle Road emerges, ultimately, from the work of the "Father of Texas," Stephen F. Austin. It was on 18 February 1823 that Stephen Austin received his first grant from the Mexican Government to establish a colony for the "Old Three Hundred." Gammel's *Laws of Texas* vol.1, page 14, has this to say about the concession:

> *As regards the limit of the Old Colony, it will be seen by reference to the concession of the emperor, of 18th February 1823, that specific limits were not considered necessary, because the colony would be composed of the lands occupied by said 300 families. The rambling disposition of the emigrants dispersed them from the east bank of the Lavaca to the east side of the San Jacinto, and from the sea shore to the upper, or San Antonio Road, and land was granted to them in those limits.*

In 1825, Austin received a second contract authorizing the settlement of five hundred additional settlers within the bounds of the first colony. It was not until 1827, after Austin had begun filling the second contract, that a definite boundary was specified for the first colony. The Mexican Government issued a proclamation in that year with the following specifications for the original colony:

The southern boundary of the first colony consisted of a line ten leagues inland, parallel to the coast, extending from the Lavaca to the west bank of the San Jacinto River. The eastern boundary would follow the San Jacinto from its intersection with this line to its source and thence due north to the San Antonio Road, which road served as the northern boundary. The western line followed the Lavaca from the ten-league juncture to its source and thence due north to the San Antonio Road. In 1828 Austin received another contract allowing him to occupy with 300 colonists, the space within the ten league line extending to the coast.

The capital of Austin's colony was San Felipe de Austin. The first signs of democratic government in Austin's Colony appeared in 1828 with the establishment of the *ayuntamiento* or council of San Felipe. This council presided over the Municipality of Austin whose authority extended, initially, over essentially the bounds incorporated within the by then three adjoining Austin colonies we have discussed of 1823, 25 and 28. Austin Municipality, then, stretched initially from the Lavaca to the San Jacinto Rivers and from the Old San Antonio Road to the coast. (There was another Austin Colony in 1827 for one hundred colonists, east of the Colorado and above the San Antonio Road—known as the "Little Colony"). In 1830, the Mexican authorities created the Precinct of Viesca reaching from the Brazos to the watershed between the San Jacinto and the Trinity. Placed under the authority of San Felipe, thus was the range of Austin Municipality stretched eastward to that same watershed, between the San Jacinto and the Trinity Rivers.

The Department of the Brazos

In 1834, the huge political entity called the Department of the Brazos was created to overlap Austin Municipality, thus extending yet further the authority of its capital, San Felipe. West to East, the dimensions of the department reached from the Lavaca River to the watershed between the San Jacinto and the Trinity Rivers. From south to north, the department extended from the Gulf much beyond the San Antonio Road, reaching all the way to the Red River.

The Department of the Brazos was the third and last department that the Mexican Government created in Texas. Having gained independence from Spain in 1821, in 1824 Mexican authorities ordered Texas united with the Mexican state of Coahuila with the capital at Saltillo, Coahuila. From 1824 until 1831, Texas consisted of one department with headquarters at San Antonio. In 1831, a second department found birth, this one to be administered from Nacogdoches. It was in order to reduce the breath of the Department of Nacogdoches in 1834 that the Mexican Government created the Department of the Brazos.

Washington Municipality created from Austin Municipality

It was to the administrator of the Department of the Brazos, James Miller, that the citizens of the northeastern portion of Austin Municipality presented two requests to form a separate municipality. The second of those requests, in 1835, is referenced below:

> *Your petitioners respectfully represent—that during the last year they did petition the Auyto [council] of the Jurisdiction of Austin to be Sepperated from said Jurisdiction and to be organized, and to form a New Jurisdiction to be called the Jurisdiction of Washington Said Petitioners set forth the limits of the said Jurisdiction and the place of holding the Corts, &c. All of which was approved of and acted upon by said Ayuto and recommended through the proper channels to the Congress of the State for its actions (as the Constitution and Laws provide) but owing to some came unknown to your petitioners the application (documents) &c was not recd by the Congress in time to be acted upon*
>
> *Your petitioners being aware of the disorganized condition of the Government of the State and of the disorder with which it is surrounded and thereby of the uncertainty of its reorganizations, deem it expedient to organize the said New Jurisdiction without any further delay. Your Petitioners being also aware of the extraordinary powers conferred upon your excellency pray that you order an organization of said Jurisdiction immediately and thereby preserve order and union amongst the Inhabitants. 2nd Day of July 1835.*

In response to this request, James Miller communicated the following directive to his successor:

Memorandum Transmitted by the Political Chief of the Department of the Brazos, James B. Miller, to His Successor in Office, Wily Martin:

San Felipe, July 19, 1835

I have permitted the jurisdiction of Washington to organize provisionally every man in the jurisdiction has signed a petition requesting said organization as their territory is extensive & this point too far, their petition passed through this Ayuntamiento to Govt and was not acted upon by the Govt last session, which caused great dissatisfaction, as soon as the Govt was again organized I intended to report them in an organized condition and pray the Govt to legalize their proceedings as every man has signed the petition for this provisional organization no man can plead to the jurisdiction of the Courts.

At least two petitions were sent to James B. Miller from the citizens of Washington. Worth Ray, in his book, *Austin Colony Pioneers*, p.33, submits that since Miller responded that "every man in the jurisdiction has signed the petition", it is apparent that at least one other petition has been lost. That would be from the citizens east of the Brazos, for none of the names of citizens from that area are listed on the known petitions. This would be the area containing, for the most part, the Cradle of Texas Road. It is to a survey of the sites and dimensions of that road that we now turn.

Selected Sources

Austin, Moses, Stephen Fuller Austin, and Eugene Campbell Barker. *The Austin Papers*. University of Texas, 1926.

Barker, Eugene Campbell. *Mexico and Texas, 1821-1835: University of Texas Research Lectures on the Causes of the Texas Revolution*. Russell & Russell, 1965.

Bugbee, Lester G. "The Old Three Hundred: A List of Settlers in Austin's First Colony." *The Quarterly of the Texas State Historical Association* 1, no. 2 (October 1, 1897): 108–117. doi:10.2307/30242636.

De Leon, Arnoldo. "Mexican Texas." In *The New Handbook of Texas*, 4:689–695. Austin: Texas State Historical Association, 1996.

Montgomery, Robin. *March to Destiny: Cultural Legacy of Stephen F. Austin's Original Colony*. Navasota: R.O.C. Press, 2010.

———. "Securing the Original Boarders of Montgomery County." In *Historic Montgomery County: An Illustrated History of Montgomery County, Texas*, 43–46. Historical Pub. Network, 2003.

Perrigo, Lynn Irwin. *Our Spanish Southwest*. Banks Upshaw, 1960.

Ray, Worth Stickley. *Austin Colony Pioneers: Including History of Bastrop, Fayette, Grimes, Montgomery, and Washington Counties, Texas*. W. S. Ray, 1949.

State, Texas (Republic). Dept. of. "Texas (Republic). Department of State: An Inventory of Department of State, Republic of Texas Election Returns at the Texas State Archives, 1835-1845." Accessed January 5, 2013. http://www.lib.utexas.edu/taro/tslac/30102/tsl-30102.html.

Texas, and D. E. Simmons. *Index to Gammel's Laws of Texas, 1822-1905…* H.P.N. Gammel, 1906.

Weber, David J. *The Mexican Frontier, 1821-1846: The American Southwest Under Mexico.* UNM Press, 1982.

Winkler, E. W. "Documents Relating to the Organization of the Muicipality of Washington, Texas." *Southwestern Historical Quarterly* 10, no. 1 (July 1906): 96–100.

CHAPTER ONE

Madisonville–Trinidad, The Green Flag Republic

The first lap of our Cradle of Texas Road celebrates an event preceding the arrival of Stephen F. Austin to Texas. Our journey begins at Madisonville at the intersection of highway 90 and the Old San Antonio Road, OSR, now highway 21. Madisonville is the county seat of Madison County, both city and town being named for the fourth president of the United States. Along the OSR from Madisonville east to the Trinity River were staged dramatic events surrounding both the birth and final demise of the 1st Republic of Texas. A marker at Midway, between Madisonville and the Trinity, tells the story succinctly. We will relay the words of the marker and then expand upon the story the marker summarizes:

Site of Trinidad

Later known as Spanish Bluff. A fort and town as early as 1805. Captured by the Magee-Gutierrez Expedition in October 1812, Near here the survivors of the Battle of Medina were executed in 1813. Inhabitants of the town were butchered by order of the Spanish commander and the town desolated.

First Declaration of the 1st Texas Republic

The full name of Trinidad was *Santisima Trinidad de Salcedo*. The Magee-Gutiérrez Expedition cited on the marker references a group of Anglo-Americans, Native Americans and *Tejanos* termed the "Republican Army of the North." While in Trinidad in October 1812, they declared Texas as a state free of Spanish control— from the Trinity to the Sabine River. By the following April, 1813, the group had conquered San Antonio, the Spanish capital of Texas. Declaring the whole state free on 6 April, they then proceeded to draw up a constitution on the 17th of that month. Truly a multicultural marvel, this, the First Republic of Texas, featured a Green Irish Flag flying over a *Tejano*-Anglo state.

Roots of the Green Flag

The foundation of the Green Flag Republic lay in the "Father of Mexico", Miguel Hidalgo's, drive to free all of Mexico from Spain. As a Lt. Colonel in Hidalgo's Army, the later president of the Green Flag Republic, Don Bernardo Gutiérrez de Lara, began his quest for freedom acting on direct instructions from Hidalgo, himself, to go the United States to secure aid. As a result, he recruited a force with US native, Augustus Magee, the originator of the green flag, at the command. Significant to these events was the wife of Don Bernardo, Doña María Joséfa de Uribe Gutiérrez. Staying behind with her family throughout the ordeal of the rise and fall of the 1st Republic of Texas, she exhibited great courage, her suffering extending to being removed from her home at the hands of Spanish authorities. Truly, Doña María was a magnificent original First Lady of Texas, although her time in the position was short.

Multicultural makeup

Significant to the story of the Green Flag Republic is its multicultural make up. The Mexican, Don Bernardo, was a citizen of a Catholic culture. His mentor, Miguel Hidalgo, had taken as his banner the image of the Virgin of Guadalupe. This image had found root in Mexico with the appearance of an apparition of the Virgin Mary to Juan Diego, an Aztec, in 1531, at the shrine of Tonantzin, the Aztec mother goddess. Following the apparition's directive, Juan Diego attempted to convince the local Catholic authorizes of the miraculous occurrence. Upon his failure here, he followed her orders to present to the authorities roses wrapped within a blue cape. It was in January and roses had never been at the shrine at that time of year. However, there they were and Juan Diego did as the apparition demanded. Upon presenting them however, instead of roses in the cape there was an image of the virgin. Thus was born what would become overtime the *Patroness of the Americas*, and the fundamental national symbol of Mexico.

Even with this strong Catholic heritage behind him, Don Bernardo yet recruited an army of citizens from the United States, a nation with Anglo-Protestant roots. Not only were those roots Protestant, but they were riding the crest of a Second "Great Religious Awakening." Exhibiting, therefore, a grand degree of togetherness, the group also picked up, along the way, a substantial cadre of Native Americans and a few African-Americans. Together, the assemblage worked its way from Louisiana to San Antonio, winning every major battle en route. On 4 August 1813, Don Bernardo Gutiérrez de Lara was forced to yield the leadership of the Green Flag Republic to José Álvarez Toledo. Only when this change in their government brought a realignment of their politics and army, isolating the units according to race, did the Army of the 1st Republic lose a major battle.

The Pivotal Battle of Medina

Awesome was that loss; the *Battle of Medina* on 18 August 1813 marked the most disastrous defeat ever on Texas soil. As implied on the marker cited above, after the battle Spanish troops under the command of Colonel Ignacio Elizondo pursued the remnants of the escaping Texas Army. Establishing his headquarters between the area of present Madisonville and the Trinity, Elizondo directed his forces to execute with impunity most of the Texas Patriots they managed to apprehend. In the process, they also demolished the very town of Trinidad to the extent that its exact location is yet a matter of dispute.

The great lesson of the First Republic of Texas, torn as it was by disastrous dissension at the Battle of Medina, is "united we stand, divided we fall." (See supplement two, for a feature article and bibliography on the 1st Republic)

Remember the Alamo

Besides its association with the area where Texas was first declared a free republic, the Madisonville area is fascinating for other reasons. For example, a Madison County man, Major W.C. Young, is credited with originating the battle cry, "Remember the Alamo!" Other Texans took up the cry as they engaged the pivotal battle for the independence of Texas at the Battle of San Jacinto.

A Texan's Texas Town

Madisonville is a real Texan's cattle town. In the 1950's and 60's, Madison County boasted more cattle per acre than other county in Texas. The famous Sidewalk Cattleman's Association event, celebrated in late May and early June, proffered the idea that Madisonville had too many "sidewalk cowboys." If one wore boots but did not own cows, he would be dumped into the horse trough on the square. Specifically, so the legend goes, should one have at least one cow, one was allowed to wear one pants leg tucked inside a boot. It took the ownership of at least two or more cows to warrant having both pants legs tucked in.

The Mushroom Festival

Another major event of the year is the famous *Mushroom Festival*, complete with a dinner the evening before a full Saturday of fun and games and, of course, delicious culinary treats. The festival is in late October.

Bucareli

Between Madisonville and the Trinity outside of Midway is another marker to an event with impact on the area of the Cradle Road. This is the story of a settlement called *Bucareli*. The story begins with the Spanish moving the capital of Texas from Los Adaes, in present Louisiana, to San Antonio in 1773. As a consequence, many settlers from East Texas were forced to move west to the new seat of government.

Some of those removed became unhappy with their new surroundings and appealed to the Spanish Viceroy Antonio Maria de Bucareli to allow them to move closer to the area of their original homes. The appeal being successful, they established a community at the junction of San Antonio Road and the Trinity River. The thankful colonists named the community Nuestra Señora del Pilar de Bucareli. This was in September 1774 and the citizens were given a ten-year waiver of taxes.

Things went seemingly well until 1777 when an epidemic apparently stemming from contaminated water, in conjunction with raids by the Comanche's in the following year, doomed the settlement. The inhabitants consequently abandoned Bucareli, to found the town of Nacogdoches. (See *Indians and Pioneers of Original Montgomery County, 25-26*)

On highway 21 four miles east of Midway, just west of the Trinity and hence in original Montgomery County territory, is a marker which reads as follows:

> *Bucareli: In this vicinity, at Paso Tomas on the Trinity, was the Spanish town Nuestra Senora del Pilar De Bucareli (1774-1779). Indian troubles had caused Spain to move Louisiana cólonists to Bexar [San Antonio]. These people, however, fled to return to East Texas, and secured the consent of Viceroy Antonio Maria Bucareli. Led by Gil Ybardo (1729-1809), they built at the Trinity crossing a church, plaza and wooden houses, and grew to a town of 345 people. But ill luck with crops, a few Comanche raids, and river floods sent the settlers farther east. Again led by Ybardo, they rebuilt the old town of Nacogdoches, 1779.*

The epidemic mentioned in the marker not only played a pivotal role in the history of citizens of Bucareli. It also led to the loss of perhaps half of the Native American tribe known as the Bidai (Bee Dye), marking the demise of that great tribe as a major player in Texas history. We turn now to more on that story.

Selected Sources

Bolton, Herbert. *Texas in the Middle Eighteenth Century: Studies in Spanish Colonial History and Administration*. New York: Russell & Russell, 1962.

Epperson, Jean. *Lost Spanish Towns: Atacosito and Trinidad De Salcedo*. 2nd ed. Houston: Kemp & Company, 2009.

Madison County Historical Commission. *A History of Madison County, Texas*. Dallas: Taylor, 1984.

Montgomery, Robin. *Indians & Pioneers in Original Montgomery County: By Robin Montgomery*. Historical Pub. Network, 2006.

CHAPTER TWO

Bedias, Original Native Americans

Moving south from Madisonville on Highway 90 we come to Bedias, named for the Native American Tribe of that name, also referred to as the Bidai. The Bedias claimed to be the original tribe of Texas and the leaders of the whole area. At the time the Europeans began to occupy Texas, their main range was between the Brazos and Trinity Rivers, west to east, and from Spring Creek to the Old San Antonio Road, south to north—the range of the whole Cradle of Texas Road. However, their range once extended far to the east of the Trinity. For example, they were allied to the Caddo, and were the builders of the great Caddo Mounds of East Texas.

A distinctive feature of the Bidai was their shaman, considered by all their neighbors as possessed of awesome supernatural power. It was believed that the shaman could assume the form of an owl and visit alien campfires, casting spells for good or evil.

The Bidai were a tribe of diplomats, maneuvering between various warring factions of Texas history, both among the Native Americans, themselves, and the French, Spanish and Anglo-Americans. So adept were they at games of intrigue that they were once trusted with a position within which they could have completely undermined the Spanish goals in Texas. This was in the early seventeen seventies, just before the epidemic at Bucareli mentioned above, which decimated their ranks.

Saga of the Triple Alliance:

In the late eighteenth century, the Spanish had initiated a reversal in their Indian policy. Part of the new policy hinged on building alliances against the Apaches, with whom they had found it futile to build an effective friendship.

As a means toward implementing the policy they sought to maneuver the Bidai into drawing upon their close relations with the Hasinai Caddo to set the stage for an alliance with the Indians of north, the Norteños, and with the Comanche's. The Caddo, however, much like the Bidai, had been driven to despise the Spanish mission system. With their sufficient agricultural system and independence of mind, the Hasinai had not succumbed in great numbers to the machinations of the Spanish seeking to place them in the missions, making of them docile neophytes.

Hence the Hasinai or Tejas (Texas) and the Bidai entered into a conspiracy to bring the Apache into a three-way alliance with them. Such a three-way confederacy would be a major counterweight to the Spanish desires. The Spanish had not yet solidified their projected alliance neither with the Norteños nor with the Comanche's; the alliance was yet in a formative, if not dream state. A solid three-way confederacy against Spanish interests would be a threat of major proportions. *(See Indians and Pioneers of Original Montgomery County, p23-25)*

In his book, *Doomed Road of Empire, (p.148)* Hodding Carter gets to the heart of the matter:

> *Now came intrigue. Governor Ripperda [of Spanish Texas] learned that the Apaches feared the treaties being signed by the Nations of the North would produce a coalition, which might seek to destroy them. Through the Bidais, a separate tribe who lived south of the camino real [San Antonio Road] and to whom they had long traded horses for guns as intermediaries, the Apaches suggested to the Texas that the three nations meet for an alliance of their own...Let the Apaches unite with the Bidais and the Texas, and they in turn with the Nations of the North, and Spain would not have the power to protect the presidios of Texas or even Coahuila itself. Something would have to be done."*

Hodding Carter further stated, "When Mézieres [Spanish liaison to the Native Americans of Texas] learned in Natchitoches that four Apache chiefs and their bands were on their way to the Texas and the Bidais Indians to draw up the proposed treaty, he had no time to lose." The Spanish were bent upon exerting maximum pressure on the Bidai and Hasinai to abort their scheme. Fortunate were the Spanish that there had been a long history of bad relations between these two eastern tribes with their would-be Apache ally upon which to build and manipulate them.

The Spanish therefore, through guile, cunning and promises, were able to prevail, preventing the consummation of the treaty. We once more turn to Hodding Carter, who wrote that the Spanish convinced the Bidai and the Texas that they "they should never forget that the Apaches were truly their enemies and must be treated as such."

The two Eastern tribes obviously were drawn to the Spanish position as shown in the following quote from Carter (p.149):

When the Apache chiefs entered [the] tent they were attacked by Texas tribesmen. Three Apache were slain. The Bidais danced over the dead bodies. Thus was the potentially dangerous alliance among the Apaches, the Texas and the Bidai avoided. At Natchitoches, Mass was said and the Te deum sung in the new parish church, resplendent in its glittering silver ornaments, for the success of Spanish arms and the beneficial results of the tour of Captain de Mézieres.

Given the Bidai's historic penchant for intrigue, their extended geographical range over the course of their history and the uncertainty of the roots of their language, an enticing possibility presents itself. The background to this thesis rests with a book, which the Naylor Company published in 1967 entitled *Latest Aztec Discoveries.* The author, Guy E. Powell, a former naval commander, makes an interesting case for the location of the original home of the Aztecs and Toltecs, and for an early home for the Mayas. Powell takes the position that all three of these great civilizations made their way to what would become the country of Mexico from an area in East Texas that could surely encompass the range the Bidai claimed for themselves, claims which the Caddo confirmed. Could the Bidai be descendants of one or all of these great civilizations?

The epicenter of this early abode of three significant tribes ranged, according to Powell, from about present Trinity to Groveton, Texas generally encompassing Trinity County. This was the land to which the Aztecs referred as Aztlan, known as the "white place" for the type of rocks in the area.

At the outset, let it be understood that there are many arguable positions on the location from which the great Mexican civilizations sprung. All have their supporters and doubters. One of the more remarkable of these suppositions is derived from a map by the great explorer and geographer, Alexander von Humboldt. In 1810,

Humboldt's map depicted Aztlan far to the north. Amongst its notable features, Humboldt's map preserves the tradition that the Aztecs migrated to Mexico from the land of Aztlan, usually referenced as a mysterious place which the Spanish thought was located near the Great Salt Lake in modern Utah.

Powell bases his claim for Trinity County and its environs as the true location for Aztlan on records from the three tribes, themselves, all of which claim to have made their way to Mexico from the north. They also describe, in common, several traits of this far distant land. In his book, Powell integrates forty-four points in favor of his designated site for Aztlan. Since there is no consensus among the scholarly community on the location of Aztlan, however, we are still left with the question, who were the Bidai really?

Echo from the prehistoric distant past

Even before the Bidai made the scene, a prehistoric event touched the latter town-site of Bedias by way of a heavenly occurrence. Thirty four million years ago, scientists tell us, a huge stone from outer space crashed to the earth under what is now Chesapeake Bay. The ferocious impact of the crash vaporized many of the rocks in the earth's crust sending them flying through the air. So great was the velocity of the flying rocks that they cooled to a glassy form before falling back to earth. In 1936, an unusual type of rock was found in Bedias and sent to the University of Texas for testing. Later, scientists surmised that this was one of those rocks launched from the pre-historic crash site under Chesapeake Bay. This type of black "tektite" is known to science as "Bediasite."

The Lady of the Lone Star

There is also a link of the town of Bedias to the lone star symbol of Texas, through Sarah Bradley Dodson. Born to a family a part of Stephen F. Austin's Old Three Hundred, she later married Archelaus Dodson and made a flag for his unit in the Texas Army of 1835. This flag preceded and provided a model for the later official Lone Star Flag. Meanwhile Sarah's flag, it is believed, flew over the building at Washington-on-the-Brazos during the convention that declared Texas an independent nation. The flag of this gracious lady received recognition in 2002 as the official Grimes County Banner. Sarah Bradley Dodson rests in peace in Bethel Cemetery near Bedias. (Standifer)

Bedias, a fascinating community with an intriguing past, is the site of a state marker that reads as follows:

Town of Bedias:

Named for North and South Bedias creeks, which in turn were named for the Bidai Indians, an agricultural people reputed to have been the oldest inhabitants of the area. Bidai means brushwood, which may refer to the building material used in their dwellings. The first white settlement in this vicinity was founded 1835 by Thomas P. Plaster, and for a while it was called Plasterville. In 1903, the community of Old Bedias surrendered most of its population to New Bedias after a branch of the International & Great Northern Railroad was built to the northeast. Townspeople from Pankey and Cotton also moved here. The name Bedias was retained, but only after a heated struggle in which determined citizens refused to have the town named for a railroad official. A famous, early resident of the Bedias area was Sarah Dodson, who in 1835 made the first Lone Star flag in Texas. She lived here from 1844 to 1848 and is buried in Old Bethel Cemetery, seven miles west. One of the most unique features of this region is the large number of Tektites (also called Bediasites) found here. These are beautiful, glassy, meteor-like stones, which fell to earth 34 million years ago. Amazingly, Indians called them jewels of the moon.

Dr. Mackie Bobo-White

Numerous are the citizens of Bedias who are active in promoting its rich cultural heritage. Standing with these citizens is the mayor, Dr. Mackie Bobo-White, helping set the tone that permeates the whole community, from representatives of the bank to the library, local businesses and the city council. Besides serving as president of the Bedias "Friends of the Library", the mayor is an educational consultant to a variety of school administrators.

Denise Upchurch

Recently named chair of the Grimes County Historical Commission is Denise Upchurch, wife of the president of the Bedias bank, Robert Upchurch. With a record of great interest and productivity in local history endeavors, great things are in store for Grimes County and by extension, the Cradle of Texas Road, under the leadership of Denise Upchurch.

Selected Sources

Carter, Hodding. *Doomed Road of Empire: The Spanish Trail of Conquest.* McGraw-Hill, 1963.

Montgomery, Robin. *Indians & Pioneers in Original Montgomery County: By Robin Montgomery.* Historical Pub. Network, 2006.

Powell, Guy E. *Latest Aztec Discoveries: Origin and Untold Riches.* Naylor Company, 1970.

Standifer, Mary. "Dodson, Sarah Randoph Bradley." In *Handbook of Texas,* 2:668. Austin: Texas State Historical Association, 1996.

CHAPTER THREE

Roans Prairie, Leadership of Washington Municipality

Joshua Hadley

At the junction of highway 90 and 30 we come to Roans Prairie. Here is the site of the home of Joshua Hadley. When Washington Municipality was formed in 1835, Josh Hadley became its *Alcalde*, a term directly translated as magistrate or mayor. However, in this case the more equivalent term is president or director. Hadley's home in present Roans Prairie saw use on occasion as a fort, providing protection during Indian attacks. The most dramatic of these occasions center on the misfortunes of a lady named Taylor.

Saga of Mrs. Taylor

On 8 March 1837, two friends, Levi Taylor and Alex Whitaker, were cow hunting near the Hadley home. Suddenly, a band of Indians surprised them taking the life of Levi while Alex escaped to tell the tale. Seeking safety for her family in the wake of the tragedy, Levi's wife, whose first name has been lost to history, accepted an invitation to move in with the Hadley's.

On 2 June 1837, Indians attacked the Hadley home. Shortly thereafter, against the pleas of the Hadley's, Mrs. Taylor rushed with her three children toward the nearby home of the venerable Joseph L. Bennett, recently a Lt. Colonel at the Battle of San Jacinto. Seizing the opportunity, the Indians again attacked, killing not only Mrs. Taylor, but also her little girl while wounding one of her two sons. Nor did the tragic scene subside with these events, for in her dying moments Mrs. Taylor conceived yet another child. The evidence available suggests that neither did that child survive.

Though weary from continual war and strife surrounding the recent war for Texas's Independence, with compassion citizens responded. Even while plans were being made to place the remaining Taylor children with their father's brother in Tennessee, others sought immediately to punish the perpetrators of the tragedy. A man named Kindred quickly sat his horse the some thirty-five miles eastward to the village of Montgomery. Comparisons to the proverbial ride of Paul Revere are certainly in order for Mr. Kindred arrived in Montgomery, secured the services of twenty-five intrepid souls and with them, returned to Hadley's Prairie—the night of the morning he had left.

The next morning the men embraced the great pursuit, traveling several hundred miles to the north. After a valiant effort they surprised the Indians who, however, managed to escape, though leaving behind their weapons and the spoils of their raid.

(There are four versions of the date and conditions of Mrs. Taylor's death. Cited here was that of Zuber. But Wilbarger states the incident occurred in 1836, Morrill in 1839 and Blair in 1840. See bibliography. Also see Robin Montgomery, *Indians and Pioneers of Original Montgomery County*, p36-38))

The Jacob Austin Band

Occupying the site of the old Joshua Hadley homestead is the Austin family, Father, David, Mother, Liz, and son, Jacob. Known as the Jacob Austin Band, the family has won multiple awards with its music. Most recently, Jacob won the national Traditional Country Music Association Mandolin Contest. The Austin's are not only musicians; they are also historians, very interested in the unique history of their home place.

The Jacob Austin Band, a scintillating component of the Cradle of Texas Road.

Founding of Roans Prairie

About 1841, Willis I Roan moved from Alabama to the vicinity of Hadley's Prairie. With a large contingent of slaves, Roan constructed a substantial log house, and began the operation of a general merchandise store. In 1849, he became the settlement's postmaster. Soon a stage route from Huntsville to San Antonio passed through the town with the community hosting a stage depot. A noted landmark, still in operation, is the Oakland Church, organized in 1854.

Red Top & the Confederacy

From Roans Prairie, a short drive to the east along highway thirty will reveal some interesting sites for the lover of Texas history. At First, should one stay on the highway, passing through the little community of Shiro for maybe a ten mile detour, one will arrive at an area once called Prairie Plains. There one will find a cemetery by the name of Red Top. Here many Confederate soldiers are at rest, and here history was made.

On 7 May 1861, Company H of the famous "Hood's Texas Brigade" was born. The organizer of the company was Proctor P.

Porter, an attorney in the town of Montgomery. His initial duty lay in mustering recruits in Montgomery County. Upon filling his quota in Montgomery, he met at Red Top with squads organized by James T. Hunter of Walker County and Thomas M. Owens of Grimes County. The assemblage chose Porter be its captain with Hunter to serve as first lieutenant and Owens as second lieutenant. Then, by way of Brenham, the tri-county company made its way to Houston and thence to Virginia. It was in Richmond, Virginia that company H became part of Hood's Texas Brigade. Units from Texas in the brigade were the First, Fourth and Fifth Texas infantry regiments. Company H was part of the Fourth Texas. These were the only Texas troops to fight in the Eastern Theater. (See *Gandy, A History of Montgomery County, TX*)

About Travis's line in the sand at the Alamo

Upon leaving Red Top and engaging the return route to highway 90 yet another treat is in store. Just across the tracks at Shiro, turn south then drive about a mile and a half. This brings you in viewing range of the site that harbored the source of an event famous across the nation. For here was revealed the story of William B. Travis drawing the line in the sand at the Alamo. Let's hear the tale:

It was on 3 March 1836. With overwhelming force, Mexican President and General Santa Anna surrounded the Alamo at San Antonio. Inside that mission complex, Commander of Texan forces, Colonel William B. Travis, addressed the situation. It appeared hopeless. Inevitable, was impending defeat. Accordingly, Travis assembled his men and, taking his sword, drew a line in the sand. "Those who wish to stay, cross this line," he commanded. All 190 fighting men in the Alamo stepped across.

Or did they? Was this whole scene just the figment of someone's imagination? The truth rests on several factors. Key to these is the veracity of William Zuber. On 6 March 1836 when the Alamo fell with the consequent death of all the Texan combatants, William Zuber was with Sam Houston's Army preparing for what turned out to be the decisive battle for Texas' Independence at San Jacinto. Thirty-seven years later, William Zuber would put into print the story of Travis drawing the line.

The next factor to consider is the source of Zuber's information as this adds yet another twist to the story. For Zuber wrote that not every fighting man in the Alamo crossed the line on that fateful day. A Frenchman named Moses Rose refused to cross. Rather, Rose slipped away over the wall into the night, to eventually find rest and sustenance in the home of William Zuber's parents, living just south of Shiro. William Zuber's father, Abraham Zuber, later to become the first district clerk of original Montgomery County, was an old friend of Moses Rose, having known him in Nacogdoches before the Texas Revolution.

Nestled in security with old friends, Rose revealed the saga to which William Zuber fell heir on his return from San Jacinto. Rose related how on the way to the Zuber's he had told the story one time to a bitter end, leading to his being labeled an imposter, the "Coward of the Alamo." Was it, therefore, in order to protect the reputation of his father's friend while he lived that Zuber waited until 1873 to put the story in print? Sources vary on Zuber's motives for waiting.

Following is William Zuber's account of Rose's meeting with his father and mother (*from the Zuber Papers*):

> *When Rose came in, my father was frightened and said, 'Rose, is this you or your ghost?' [The elder Zuber thought that Rose had died in the Alamo]. Rose arrived in a pitiful condition: .. thorns had worked very deep into his flesh and rendered him so lame that he walked in much pain and his steps were short*

and slow. Rose remarked to my father that it was he and not his ghost, of course, he was feverish and sick, moreover, he had not changed his apparel since leaving the Alamo. My father supplied him with a clean suit and my mother had a servant to wash his clothes. When the servant had opened the wallet [of clothes] the first garments that she took out were those which had fallen out in the puddle of blood thrown from the wall of the Alamo, and the clotted blood which had dried in the wallet, had glued them together. My parents occupied part of two or three days picking thorns from his legs with a pair of nippers. My mother made a supply of salve which being daily applied to sores healed them rapidly. After resting a few days and becoming easy Rose dispensed for a time with his reticence and related freely to my parents the history of the escape, the circumstances connected therewith, and his travel from the Alamo to their house at their request; he repeated it often till my mother could repeat it as well as he.

Whatever one's view of Rose, it should be borne in mind that most sources agree that Moses Rose had fought bravely under Napoleon as the latter sought to become the ruler of Europe. Furthermore, Rose fought in three battles in Texas preliminary to the Alamo. Should Zuber's story of Rose leaving the Alamo ring true, it seems clear that Rose did not leave because he was a coward.

Standing near the scene of so much will put one in a reflective mood, as the path to Roans Prairie is re-traced in preparation to drive to the next stop of the Cradle Road.

Selected Sources

Blair, A. L. *Early History of Grimes County.* Austin, 1930.

Gandy, William Harley. *A History of Montgomery County, Texas*, 1952.

Montgomery, Robin. *Indians & Pioneers in Original Montgomery County: By Robin Montgomery.* Historical Pub. Network, 2006.

Morrell, Z. N. *FLOWERS AND FRUITS FROM THE WILDERNESS.* Boston: Gould and Lincoln, 1872.

Wilbarger, John Wesley. *Indian Depredations in Texas: Reliable Accounts of Battles, Wars, Adventures, Forays, Murders, Massacres, Etc., Etc., Together with Biographical Sketches of Many of the Most Noted Indian Fighters and Frontiersmen of Texas.* Steck co, 1889.

Zuber, William Physick. "A Guide to the Zuber (William Physick) Papers, Ca. 1820-1923." Accessed January 5, 2013. http://www.lib.utexas.edu/taro/utcah/03199/cah-03199.html.

"Hood's Texas Brigade." 3:687. Austin: Texas State Historical Association, 1996.

CHAPTER FOUR

Anderson, and Statehood

In memory of Kenneth Anderson

Continuing south from Roans Prairie on 90 we come to Anderson. Originally the community was called Alta Mira or sometimes Fanthorp, the latter for the fine home of Henry Fanthorp, which home still stands much as it was during the era of the Republic of Texas, 1836-45. To Fanthorp Inn in the summer of 1845 came Kenneth Anderson. As the last vice president of the Republic of Texas, Anderson had just presided over the ceremony at Washington-on-the-Brazos wherein the Texas Legislature applied for admission as a state of the Union. At Fanthorp Inn, Anderson died and was interred across the street. Shortly thereafter, the community assumed the name of Anderson, in celebration of Texas becoming a state.

Following is the wording of the state marker at Anderson's gravesite:

ANDERSON

Erected by the State of Texas In memory of

KENNETH LEWIS ANDERSON

Born in Hillsboro, North Carolina, Sept. 11, 1805

District Judge, Speaker of the House of the Sixth Congress And last Vice President of the Republic of Texas Died July 3, 1845

The name of the town of Fanthorp was changed to Anderson in his honor

A religious first in Texas

In 1834, seven members of the Pilgrim Regular Predestinarian Baptist Church of Illinois held their first religious service in Texas, in the community of later Anderson. This was probably the first Baptist Church service in Texas history. Furthermore, the pastor of Pilgrim Church, Daniel Parker, performed the first wedding ceremony in the original Montgomery County area. In the summer of 1834, he married Henry Fanthorp and Rachel Kennard in their future home. (*See Saga of Anderson*)

Grimes County Seat

In 1846, Grimes County emerged, breaking off from Montgomery County. Anderson, then the major town of the county, became the county seat, a title that it still holds. In the middle of the main street is one of the most picturesque courthouses in the state. So unusual is it that it was once placed in the famous syndicated newspaper piece, "Ripley's Believe it or not."

Following is a state historical marker referencing the building:

Grimes County Courthouse, Anderson, TX, USA:

Unique Victorian Texas public building. Third courthouse here. Site, in an 1824 land grant from Mexico, was donated 1850 by Henry Fanthorp, first permanent settler in county. Built 1891 of hand-molded brick with native stone trim. Vault is same one used in previous buildings, has twice withstood fires. Tried here in 1930s, a Clyde Barrow gang member vowed he'd see court in infernal regions. Recorded Texas Historic Landmark, 1965.

The great shootout of 1900

At this courthouse in the first year of the twentieth century was one of Texas's most dramatic shootouts. The basis for the event traces to the close of the Civil War. Upon returning home from the war in May 1865, some Confederate veterans congregated in Navasota. Disconcerted over the war generally and over the withholding of their pay, they looted a warehouse filled with cotton and munitions. In the process a fire and great explosion demolished several nearby buildings, leaving devastated much of the town's commercial district.

The consequent placement of federal troops at nearby Anderson as well as Millican to the north led to further violence, most of it white against black. Hence the Freedmen Bureau entered Grimes County to support African-Americans with the franchise, court and labor business and with education. This, in turn, led to further violence including the rise of the Ku Klux Klan. Action generating re-action, local African-Americans formed their own militias interspersed with chapters of secrecy-laden loyal or Union Leagues.

A primary catalyst to African-American strength was numbers. By 1870, that race constituted some 60% of the county's population. The loyalty of African-American voters, therefore, enabled the republicans to retain considerable influence in the county throughout the rest of the 19th century. Not only numbers of African-Americans was significant in the measuring of republican power, but also credit and market difficulties spawned agrarian radicalism in Grimes County. As a result, by the 1880s, poorer white farmers allied with African-Americans to form a People's Party of populist orientation.

So greatly did the populist alliance alarm the conservative establishment that it led to the shootout on the main street of Anderson on 7 November 1900. In the melee, populist sheriff, Garret Scott, lay wounded while his deputy and brother, Emmett Lee Scott, suffered death at the hands of William McDonald. McDonald also lost his life, however, as did a bystander, J. L. Bradley. Only the timely arrival of armed militia ushered in by rail from Houston via Navasota enabled the wounded sheriff to escape with his life for medical treatment elsewhere. This shootout held far-ranging consequences as it brought into the open the "White Man's Union" which would control Grimes County Politics until the 1950s. *(See* for instance, *Navasota: Images of America)*

Tribute to a Bridge

Among the historical and unique treasures of Anderson is an historic bridge in the central park. Active in promoting the project was the *Anderson Historical Society* composed of visionaries active in preserving and promoting the rich history and culture of the town. Among those active in the society is the dynamic mayor, Gail Sowell.

The marker near the historic bridge tells its story:

> *This historic bridge was originally located on CR 263 (known locally as CR 180) over Rocky Creek. Constructed around 1905, the Warren pony truss measures 50 feet in length and is a rare survivor of a once-common structure. The single-span, four-panel bridge is comprised primarily of riveted and bolted steel channels, I-beams and plates and pin-connected Eye-bars. The main steel*

components were shop-riveted and then bolted in to their final configuration on site.

A popular retreat through the 1890s, nearby Kellum Springs was likely a motivating force that resulted in the development of an early road north of Anderson that led to the springs and then connected with Iola to facilitate travel from the northern reaches of the county. The crossing of Rocky Creek with a bridge along this route was a necessity, as it remained a primary north/south route between Anderson and Iola into the 20th century.

The bridge now stands as an early landmark of Texas engineering history with a heritage proudly shared by the people of Grimes County.

A major Confederate Command Post

A significant legacy of the Civil War in Grimes County was played out some seven miles northwest of Anderson. Though it boggles the imagination to think of it, here on a now rather desolate piece of earth once stood the elegant Piedmont Springs Resort, once instrumental in the broader Confederate military strategy. On the grounds of the resort were three flowing sulphur springs supporting several bathhouses and a four-story one hundred-room hotel. Here guests enjoyed billiards, poker and even betting on a favorite pastime of the era, horseracing. In the opulent ballroom of the hotel the elite of the region including, local legend says, Sam Houston, danced the minuet.

The majestic hotel was constructed in 1860. It was during the summer of 1863 that the hotel was of service to General John Bankhead Magruder, commander of the Confederate Military District encompassing Texas, New Mexico and Arizona. It was this situation that made Piedmont Springs, for a time, the de facto headquarters of that huge military district. General Magruder had been instrumental in liberating Galveston from Union troops in January 1863. Later, in 1865, the ballroom of the hotel became a military hospital for General John G. Walker's Greyhound Division.

Following is a state marker to this site:

Site of Piedmont Springs Resort:

In operation as early as 1850 as health spa and resort because of three nearby sulphur springs (varying in taste from mild to strong). Numerous drinking places and bathhouses allowed guests to move freely about grounds. Grand four-story hotel with 100 rooms, built about 1860, was social center for area, where guests enjoyed billiards, poker, horse races, and General Sam Houston once danced the Minuet. In 1865, hotel became hospital, headquarters for John G. Walker's Greyhound Division, Confederate Army. Owner closed the building after losing money in panic, 1870s. Recorded Texas Historic Landmark, 1967.

Back to Anderson and ten miles east on FM 149 leads to Richards, Texas, the home of the Texas Center for Regional Studies.

Selected Sources

Allen, Irene Taylor. *Saga of Anderson: The Proud Story of a Historic Texas Community*. Greenwich Book Publishers, 1958.

Commission, Grimes County Heritage. *History of Grimes County Texas: Heritage and Progress*. The Commission, 1982.

Jackson, Charles Christopher. "Grimes County." In *Handbook of Texas*, 3:342–347. Austin: Texas State Historical Association, 1996.

Montgomery, Robin, Joy Montgomery, and Texas Center for Regional Studies. *Navasota*. Arcadia Publishing, 2012.

CHAPTER FIVE

Navasota, Birth of the Cradle Concept

At Navasota, highway 90 merges into highway 105. It was near here, on 19 March 1687 that René Robert Cavelier Sieur de La Salle met his death. The community supports two statues celebrating the event. On 5 May 2012 Navasota hosted a *Texas Legacy Celebration* featuring the rededication of a statue of La Salle with a marker from the French. The lettering on the French marker is presented below:

> *Rene Robert Cavelier, Sieur De La Salle (1643-1687) French Explorer and Founder of the First European Colony in Texas, Fort St. Louis near Lavaca Bay, in the year 1685. He was assassinated by some of his own men, probably, at a site near the present town of Navasota, Texas in March 1687.*
>
> *This bust given to the people of Navasota by the FRENCH COMMITTEE FOR THE BICENTENNIAL OF THE*

INDEPENDENCE OF THE UNITED STATES AND THE ASSOCIATION FRANCE-AMERIQUE to commemorate the 333rd anniversary of the Explorer's birth in Rouen, France.

November 22, 1976

In a large sense, La Salle was the true originator of Texas. This story begins in 1682 when La Salle led an expedition from Canada down the Mississippi to the Gulf of Mexico. There he claimed all the land draining the mighty river for his native France. He then named that vast area Louisiana for his sovereign King Louis XIV and his wife, Anne. On returning to France, he secured another expedition to return to Louisiana. En route, he lost both his way and his ships, and became stranded off the shores of Matagorda Bay. From here, various forays were made seeking to find the Mississippi.

La Salle failed to find the great river, even losing his life on his last try, as already mentioned near present Navasota. But the French presence north of the Rio Grande had placed fear in the hearts of the Spanish then in control of Mexico. Accordingly, they not only, after several tries, found the remains of La Salle's headquarters called Fort Saint Louis, near the bay. In 1690, the year after the find, the Spanish also sent an expedition beyond the Trinity River, blazing en route the La Bahia Trail from Matagorda to the Trinity. Once beyond that stream they established a mission that they named *San Francisco de las Tejas*. The word *Tejas* came from the Caddo Indian word *Tayshas*. These words in English may be translated as Texas, meaning friend.

Though the Spanish soon abandoned the Tejas mission, in the seventeen twenties they established east of the Trinity the Province of Texas, later in 1773 moving the capital to San Antonio. All this was initiated because La Salle's presence motivated the Spanish to make a presence east of the Trinity to keep watch on the French, then in control of Louisiana.

(for sources, see the article on La Salle, Cradle
of Texas Road Supplement, One)

In addition to the two statues of La Salle, Navasota also has the following marker to the trail that La Salle's presence inspired:

La Bahia Trail:

Originally an Indian trail through Southern Texas and Louisiana; known to Spanish explorers as early as 1690, when the De Leon Expedition passed this site on the way from Mexico to East Texas. With 115 men, 721 horses, 82 loads of flour, and other supplies, Alonso de Leon, Governor of Coahuila, and Father Massanet, a Franciscan priest, entered the wilds of Texas. The purpose of the expedition was to discourage French encroachment from the north, as well as to explore, colonize, and Christianize the Indians. They followed the rugged trail from the present town of Refugio to Goliad and continued northeast to Navasota, probably following Cedar Creek through this town. Then they journeyed north until reaching the Neches River, where (near present Weches) they founded the Mission of San Francisco de Las Tejas. The church was called after the Tejas, or Friendly Indians, whose name was eventually given to the entire state. Although de Leon' party went no farther on the western section of the trail, known as Atascosito Road, the eastern section extended into Louisiana. In the nineteenth century, the route gained importance as a cattle trail, the Opelousas Road that moved Texas herds to market in the north and east.

La Salle, then, played the key role, if inadvertently, in motivating the Spanish to forge the Bahia Trail and give birth to Texas. This is well substantiated by the facts. A related story, however, is of legendary proportions. Regardless of the ultimate veracity of its claims, the story, itself, definitely played a motivating role, along with La Salle, in blazing the Bahia Trail. Incredible as it sounds, this is the saga of a nun of the Franciscan Order who probably never left her little village in Spain.

The Bidai and the Blue Nun

Our story begins in the 1620s, before the Spanish had established a permanent presence in Texas. They were by then, though, rulers over New Mexico. During this time, Jumano Indians from West Texas traveled to New Mexico seeking Christian missionaries. Surprised, the Spanish authorities inquired as to how the Indians learned about the Christian religion. With awe in their voices, the Jumanos described a Lady in Blue, a Franciscan nun, while pointing the Spanish toward the land of the Caddo.

As we have seen in the section on the town of Bedias, the Caddo were relatives of the Bidai (Bee Dye) Indians who, by the time the Anglo-Americans came, ranged basically between the Trinity and the Brazos Rivers below the San Antonio Road. It is known that the impact of the Bidai stretched toward the heart of the Caddo domain. For it was the Caddo, themselves, who asserted to Spanish explorers that the Bidai were the builders of the huge Indian mounds of East Texas, known to history as the "Caddo Mounds." (See *Texas by Teran,* p.228)

The Caddo believed that Bidai Shamans, even as they remained bodily in their villages, could appear as owls at Caddo campfires. Thus convinced of the reality of bi-location of the body or spirit from one place to another, the Caddo were conditioned to accept the story of the Blue Nun. That story held that while never leaving her convent in Agreda, Spain, the nun bi-located to Texas to administer to multitudes of Indians in the 1620s.

It was against this background that the Spanish priests in New

Mexico received the delegation of Jumano Indians with their request for missionaries to their lands in Texas. Responding, over the next half century the Franciscans converted some 60,000 Texas Indians! The Franciscans had not yet worked their way to the land of the Caddo however when word reached Spanish authorities that the French had established a fort off Matagorda Bay.

By the time a Spanish expedition found the French establishment, in 1689, the French leader La Salle had been killed by his own men near present Navasota. With the Spanish Expedition that discovered the French fort was a Franciscan priest, Father Damien Massanet. While there, Massanet learned that the Caddo wanted the Spanish to minister to them. "Why?" the Father asked. Because a nun with a blue cape had ministered to their ancestors, came the answer. (See, for instance, Bob Bowman, "Lady in Blue")

It was during the next year, 1690, that the Spanish finally reached the land of the Caddo, establishing a mission named *San Francisco de las Tejas*. Along with the apprehension engendered from the presence of La Salle, the legend of the Blue Nun should be associated with the appellation of Cradle of Texas. (for the significance of the legend in the larger context of Texas history see *March to Destiny, p45-53*)

Mance Lipscomb & "The Blues"

In its more recent history, Navasota is the home of Mance Lipscomb, a "songster", who played a major role in giving birth to the genre known as the "Trans-Brazos Blues." Navasota is the official "Blues Capital of Texas." Annually, in August, a massive blues festival is held in Navasota, in honor of the venerable Mance Lipscomb. Furthermore, a statue to the great Lipscomb sits in a prominent place near the center of the city.

Mance Lipscomb received birth in Navasota in 1895. His surname came from slave owners of his father while Mance chose his own name as a play on the word emancipation. He took up the guitar at age eleven and soon was playing locally with his father who was a fiddler. For most of his life, Mance was a sharecropper and rarely left his hometown. He came to have a wife and son, plus three adopted children.

In the late fifties, Mance ran into problems for an altercation in which he sought to defend his wife's honor. This led to several years hiding out in Houston. It was about this time that blues historian, Chris Strachwitz, discovered his talents. The rest is history. His fans reached to the likes of Frank Sinatra.

Frank Hamer, Navasota's Answer to Wild Bill Hickok

As a youth, Lipscomb was a close friend of the marshal of the town, Frank Hamer, and purportedly referred to the marshal as "Hayman." Hamer provided law and order for Navasota from 1908-11. Later, in 1934, this Texas Ranger gained worldwide fame when he corralled the famous outlaw couple, "Bonnie and Clyde."

It was at the end of the Civil War that Navasota began the descent into social trauma, which necessitated a Frank Hamer. This was when disgruntled soldiers caused a major explosion of ammunition, igniting a terrible fire. Social unrest during the post war reconstruction period led, by the end of the nineteenth century, to a momentous shoot-out on the streets of Anderson. In that drama, Navasotans played a key role.

So chaotic were conditions in Navasota in the first decade of the twentieth century that a marshal called it quits and fled the scene after only a week in the service of the city. Not so Frank Hamer, who followed that marshal, to reign as king over the streets and saloons. Hamer established his credentials as the ruler of the town when, with his fists, he left the town bully agonizing in pain in a pile of mud.

Reflective of Frank Hamer's character was his actions during the days of the Mexican Revolution of 1910-20. Repercussions of the struggle in that nation were spilling over into the United States. In the middle years of the struggle, the Texas Rangers were called to the Texas border country to address an insurgency launched in the wake of the "Plan of San Diego." Supposedly written in the Texas border town of San Diego in January 1915, the plan called for Mexican-Americans, African-Americans and Japanese to ignite a rebellion meant ultimately to return the American Southwest to Mexican control.

Several factions in Mexico were vying for control of that country. In October 1915, the United States recognized Venustiano Carranza and placed an embargo on aid to his rivals. However, certain elites behind the scenes in the US and Texas felt that their interests were better served with Carranza's competitors for power. Accordingly, the Rangers were given the word to act as though they were policing the smuggling of arms, but in reality to ignore such practices.

This finessing of the law, Frank Hamer could not abide. Consequently, he was left virtually alone to patrol hundreds of miles of the border country. Finding his task impossible, he took the initiative to cross the border and work with the Mexican forces with whom the US was officially allied, to counter the clandestine arms trafficking from the United States. For Frank Hamer, the law would be upheld, even if it meant defying his own government. (See, for example, *Jenkins, "Hamer, Francis Augustus" and Russell Cushman, article, Navasota Examiner)*

Russell Cushman

An expert on Frank Hamer, as well as Mance Lipscomb, is Russell Cushman, a talented artist who has been commissioned to fashion a statue of Frank Hamer for the city of Navasota. Not only an artist, but twice elected to the Navasota City Council, Cushman's sculptures and historical murals are landmarks in the Brazos Valley. A 140-foot mural depicting virgin Texas in 1845, found on the second-story interior of the Republic Museum at Washington-on-the-Brazos, is arguably the most famous of his pieces.

Leon Collins and Mollie Bee

Close friends of Russell Cushman are the talented father and daughter duo, Leon Collins and Mollie Bee. Although centered on the Brazos Valley, their African-American folk art has a national reach.

Besides great artists, Navasota holds distinction as "The Town that Trains Built."

Naming of the River Navasota

We dare not close this chapter without a look at the legend which folklore holds gave the name Navasota to the river that runs near the city which is its namesake. It is said that the river's name stems from the phrase, "Nativity of Soto", roughly translated as birth of Soto. A remnant of the expedition of Hernando de Soto, about the year 1540, made an expedition, which some historians claim, reached as far as the Brazos River. En route, the legend goes, this remnant, under the command of Luis de Moscoso, sought to gain leverage over the local Native Americans by capitalizing upon their belief in the miraculous generative powers of river waters. Accordingly, Moscoso, so the story goes, convinced the Native Americans near a stream neighbor to the Brazos, that Hernando de Soto had risen rebirthed from its waters; hence the name of the stream, Navasota.

Selected Sources

Bowman, Bob. "The Lady in Blue." *Texas Escapes Online Magazine,* n.d.

Foster, William C., and Nicolas de La Salle. *The La Salle Expedition on the Mississippi River: a Lost Manuscript of Nicolas De La Salle, 1682.* Texas State Historical Association, 2003.

Jackson, Jack, Manuel de Mier y Terán, Scooter Cheatham, and Lynn Marshall. *Texas by Terán: The Diary Kept by General Manuel De Mier Y Terán on His 1828 Inspection of Texas.* University of Texas Press, 2000.

Jenkins, John. "Hamer, Francis Augustus." In *Handbook of Texas,* 3:426–427. Austin: Texas State Historical Association, 1996.

Lipscomb, Mance Alyn. "A Guide to the Lipscomb-Alyn Collection, 1960-1995." Accessed January 5, 2013. http://www.lib.utexas.edu/taro/utcah/01237/cah-01237.html.

Montgomery, Robin. *March to Destiny: Cultural Legacy of Stephen F. Austin's Original Colony.* Navasota: R.O.C. Press, 2010.

———. *Tortured Destiny: Lament of a Shaman Princess.* Christian Ages Press, 2001.

Montgomery, Robin, Joy Montgomery, and Texas Center for Regional Studies. *Navasota.* Arcadia Publishing, 2012.

Weddle, Robert S. "Moscoso Alvarado, Luis De (1505-1551)." In *Handbook of Texas,* 4:851. Austin: Texas State Historical Association, 1996.

CHAPTER SIX

Washington-on-the-Brazos, Home of the 2nd Texas Republic

Pursuant to the dream ignited with Stephen Austin's procurement of the grant for his first colony, pioneers, initially called Texians, were trickling into the designated territory of the grant as early as 1821. In that year, Andrew Robinson, accompanied by Abner, Joseph and Robert Kuykendall and their families crossed to the west side of the Brazos. Within a year, others joined them, including Thomas Boatwright, James Gray, Abner Robinson and William Gates. With so much passing, by 1822, Andrew Robinson was operating a ferry at the old La Bahia crossing. Soon thereafter, the quickly developing community assumed the name of La Bahia Settlement.

In 1831, Robinson bequeathed one-quarter league to his daughter, Patsy, and son-in-law, John W. Hall. The latter by the end of 1833 had surveyed the site and laid out a town. The first resident of the town was a Methodist Minister named John W. Kinney. In 1835, John

Hall purchased the remainder of the Robinson grant and established what he christened the Washington Town Company. His partners in the enterprise were Dr. Asa Hoxey and Thomas Gay, along with the Miller and Somerville Company. Hoxey, a former resident of the town of Washington, Wilkes County, Georgia named the new town after his hometown.

By the time it received its name, Washington-on-the-Brazos was enjoying a reputation as a supply point. Attracted by the river, the La Bahia Road and feeder roads, merchants and tradesmen were swelling the ranks of the town. In December 1835 Washington became the headquarters and concentration point for Texas's army volunteers and supplies. It was in July of that year, as we have seen, that Washington became the capital of Washington Municipality.

It was at the capital of Washington Municipality that Texians convened for seventeen days in March of 1836. There they deliberated, declared their independence from Mexico and wrote a constitution. This set the stage for the birth of the Texas Republic after the ensuing Battle of San Jacinto on 21 April 1836. Later, in June of 1845, Washington-on-the-Brazos set the scene for Texas to become a state of the Union when the legislature gave its ascent.

A state marker at Washington reads as follows:

> *This frontier village was the setting for the convention that on March 2, 1836, wrote and signed the immortal Texas Declaration of Independence in this first capital of the Republic of Texas, the first constitution was drawn, and on March 17 the government had to flee. After the Texas victory at San Jacinto, April 21, 1836, Washington was again proposed as capital, but Houston was selected instead. In 1843, the Republic's government returned to Washington and remained here during the term of Anson Jones, fourth and last president of Texas, where he at once began the practice of his profession, medicine. At the Battle of San Jacinto,*

in the Texas Revolution, he took the field as surgeon of the 2ⁿᵈ Regiment. Later he served in the Texas Congress, was minister to the United States, Secretary of State, a senator, and finally the president from 1844 to 1846. Upon annexation of Texas to the United States, Dr. Jones retired to Barrington, his plantation near Washington. He died in Houston on January 9, 1858.

Selected Sources

Christian, Carole. "Washington-on-the-Brazos, TX." In *Handbook of Texas*, 6:832–834. Austin: Texas State Historical Association, 1996.

Kemp, Louis Wiltz. *The Signers of the Texas Declaration of Independence.* The Anson Jones press, 1944.

Steen, Ralph. "Convention of 1836." In *Handbook of Texas*, 3:297. Austin: Texas State Historical Association, 1996.

CHAPTER SEVEN

Grimes and Montgomery Prairies, and Significant Pioneers

Grimes Prairie

Ten miles or so east of Navasota on 105 is the community of Stoneham. Just before reaching Stoneham Cemetery, turn north on the Farm to Market Road and drive some two miles and there on the left is "Monument Hill". Standing at the picturesque gate and peering some one hundred yards, one beholds a little wooded area. Here are remains of citizens of Grimes Prairie, and here is the site where once was interred Jesse Grimes. A signer of the Texas Declaration of Independence, Jesse Grimes was the man for whom Grimes County received its name. He served in the War of 1812 and arrived in what would become Grimes County in 1827. In 1830, the Mexican government created the District of Viesca, stretching from the Brazos to beyond the San Jacinto River. Over this area, Jesse served as lieutenant of militia, *sindico procurador, regidor,* and treasurer. During the Republic of Texas (1836-45), he served as first chief justice of Montgomery County and also represented Washington, Montgomery and Brazos Counties in the legislature. With statehood in 1846, he served four terms as state senator for Grimes County, rising to the position of senate pro tempore.

Amongst Jesse Grime's closest friends was Sam Houston. This was evidenced strongly in 1857, when Sam Houston named him as his running mate when he ran for governor against the team of Hardin Runnels for governor and Frank Lubbock for Lt. Governor. The pro union stance of Houston-Grimes was a pivotal factor costing them the election.

Earlier, in 1834, another close friend, William B. Travis, then a member of the *ayuntamiento* of Austin sent Jesse Grimes the notice of his appointment to the office of "Judge of the First Instance" of the Jurisdiction of Austin. The notice stated in part: "You will immediately repair to [San Felipe de Austin] for the purpose of being installed into your new office and taking the oaths prescribed by the Constitution and Law. All of which I communicate to you for your intelligence and compliance."(*Ben Grimes, Private Papers*)

Not only were the talents of Jesse Grimes in demand in the legal and political realm, he also was in demand as a man of military acumen. In 1835, Jesse was a delegate from Washington Municipality to the Consultation, where Henry Smith received election to the provisional governorship of Texas. While in active control of affairs of state, Smith proffered Grimes an appointment, as follows (*from Ben Grimes, private papers*):

"To Jesse Grimes Esq.,

In the name of the People of Texas, Free and Sovereign, I, reposing official trust and confidence in your patriotism, valor, conduct and fidelity, do BY THESE PRESENTS, constitute and appoint [to the] rank of Col., I being, by virtue of my office, Commander in Chief of the Army of Texas, for the defense of the republican principles of the Constitution of 1824, and for repelling every hostile invasion thereof. And we do also enjoin and require you to regulate your conduct in every respect by the rules and discipline adopted by the United State of North American in time of war, or such laws and regulations as may be adopted by this Government; and punctually to observe and follow such orders and directions, from time to time as you shall receive I do hereby strictly charge and require all officers and soldiers under your command, to be obedient to your orders, and diligent in exercise of their several duties...Done at San Felipe on the fourth day of December, Eighteen hundred and Thirty Five."

Testimony to Jesse's prowess in matters military came on the eve of the Battle of San Jacinto. On 25 March 1836, just after the Constitutional Convention had changed Mexican Municipalities into counties, President David G. Burnet, appointed Jesse to organize the militia in the huge county of Washington. This was under the provisions of an act of the convention of 12 March 1836. Burnet's orders continued, in part: "[You] will therefore proceed to the discharge of your duties under that act ordering out two thirds of the Militia of said County forthwith to serve for and during the term of three months, a prompt and energetic discharge of the duties required of you by this act is expected, the Country demands the aid of every man and it is confidentially believed that all will do their duty."(*Ben Grimes papers*)

Jesse Grimes, by two wives, Martha Smith and after her death, Rosanna Ward Britton, sired 14 children. In 1929, the remains of Jesse and Rosanna were exhumed from their resting place at Grimes Prairie and reburied with great ceremony in a place of honor in Austin.

A state marker at Anderson summarizes Jesse Grime's career while officially awarding him the title of Grimes County's namesake:

Grimes County-Named After Jesse Grimes:

Created April 6, 1846; Organized July 13, 1846; Named in honor of Jesse Grimes 1788-1866; Signer of the Texas Declaration of Independence; Member of the Texas Congress; County Seat, Anderson, originally known as Fanthorp.

Montgomery Prairie

Just east of Grimes Prairie was the community of Montgomery Prairie, named for the Montgomery clan; numerous of whose members were in the immediate area stretching east to the site of the later town of Montgomery. The earliest member of the family to arrive in Texas was Andrew Montgomery in 1820; one of the signatories of a formal document in the State Archives testifying to that fact was Jesse Grimes (See *Petition to Legislature*). It is documented also that Jesse Grimes and Andrew worked together tending for survivors of the Ft. Parker Massacre in 1836(See *Rachel Plummer Narrative*). This was just after Andrew and his brother, John, had returned from the Battle of San Jacinto.

J. G. W. Pierson

A member of the Montgomery clan was a brother-in-law, J.G. W. Pierson, who, among numerous other accomplishments, was the de facto leader of Robertson's Colony to the north of Austin Municipality. Pierson and Andrew, along with Andrew's brothers, Edley and John, had gone to Robertson's Colony with Pierson, initially with the mission of surveying Saraville de Viesca, at the time slated to become the capital of all of Texas (*History of Falls County, p22*). Andrew was named the Adjusting Surveyor. During their stay there, the area suffered the worst Indian depredations in the history of the state (*Border Wars of TX, p148*). Later Andrew and John both fought under Sam Houston at the Battle of San Jacinto.

On 13 February, 1836, Pierson received the following document from the acting governor of Texas, James Robinson, as recorded in volume nine of the official *Papers of the Texas Revolution (p156)*:

> *...it will be recalled that this district was surveyed by many of the citizens of Montgomery and Grimes Prairie.*
>
> *Believing you are willing to serve your country in any way that you can be useful and the alarming fact that the enemy force commanded by Santa Anna in person is about to attack our beloved country at all points and the unorganized and deplorable conditions of the militia calls for prompt organization, I have therefore taken the liberty to appoint you my aid-de-camp for the Municipality of Viesca. You will make all necessary purchases of supplies and provisions, ammunitions, pack horses for the men on their march to Gonzales where you will gather the men and officers and report them to the officer in command. You are empowered to do all things necessary for the defense of Texas for she must now fight, submit or fly, and I hope everyone is ready to choose the first, and if anyone wishes to serve Texas, let him do in now as others did at San Antonio where they caused the Black Flag to come down and the tyrant to implore for mercy.*

Later, in the wake of Jesse Grime's organization of the Washington County Militia, Pierson received an appointment from Sam Houston to lead said Militia. It was during this time, on his return to the area, that he named the region just north of Montgomery Prairie High Point.

Pierson, the Mier Expedition and Drawing of the Black Beans

During the days of the Texas Republic, Mexico, still cherishing the hope that she could subdue the Texans, kept up a shadow of a claim to the severed province on occasion sending invading parties into the state. One of these forays under the command of General Rafael Vasquez resulted in the occupation of San Antonio on 5 March 1842. While Vasquez remodeled the city government after the Mexican style, other forces occupied Refugio and Goliad. Finally in September a formidable force under General Adrian Woll arrived in the vicinity of San Antonio prompting President Sam Houston to call for Texan forces to address the situation.

Houston chose General Alexander Somervell to organize the Texas Army. Accordingly on 17 November 1842, Somervell organized two regiments. The commander of one of these was Joseph L. Bennett, the former Lt. Colonel from Montgomery County who had helped direct the Texans at the Battle of San Jacinto. Composing Colonel Bennett's regiment was a large contingent from the original Montgomery County. After the Texan Army arrived at its headquarters in Bexar, general restlessness and lack of supplies soon rendered it dissatisfied. This disgruntlement enveloped General Somervell who aborted his mission in December 1842, after leading his men to the Rio Grande. Many of his forces consequently took leave of the action and returned home.

One of the Texans who remained on the Rio Grande was J.G.W. Pierson, who, though forty-seven years of age, had once again raised a company to help repel the Mexicans. With Pierson on the great river were Captains Ewen Cameron and William Eastland and their companies. The now reduced Texan force elected William Fisher to the command, and then proceeded to drive the Mexican troops into the Mexican town of Mier. During the engagement Colonel Fisher was wounded prompting one of his men to raise a white flag. Thinking this meant surrender, Texans began to stack their arms. Seizing the opportunity, the Mexicans captured the Texans on this 26th day of December 1842 and marched them to Saltillo. En route, the Texans overpowered the Mexican guard at Hacienda Salado and recovered their arms, mules, wagons and camp equipage.

At this point they paused to choose a commander. The prime candidates, Cameron and Pierson, espoused opposing strategy. The former favored taking to the mountains, while the latter thought the route by the public roads to be more fortuitous. Cameron won, and they took to the mountains where they soon became lost, ran out of provisions and yielded quietly to a Mexican patrol that took them to Salado.

Upon their arrival at Salado, the officers were placed in separate cells from the men. A Mexican woman who furnished meals to Pierson told him that every 10th man was condemned to be shot. She said that each Texan would be blindfolded, after which he would draw a bean from a jar. Those drawing a white bean would live while the unfortunates who retrieved black ones would be shot. The woman gave Pierson information that probably saved his life: the black beans were rough, while the white ones were slick.

Captain Cameron was the first person to be blindfolded and placed before the jar containing seventeen black beans and 159 white ones. Unfortunately, Cameron was also the first to draw a black bean. It was rumored that he drew a white bean but was ordered shot anyway. Captain Eastland was next and also drew a black bean. At the end of this gruesome ceremony on 25 April 1843, the seventeen drawing black beans were marched out and shot one at a time, in the presence of their comrades.

The members of the Mier expedition, including Pierson, who were fortunate enough to draw a white bean, were marched to Perote Prison in Central Mexico where they joined many of the survivors of other Texan expeditions. Eventually, Pierson managed to make his way back to his beloved High Point. (*Crittenden Papers*)

The community of Stoneham is on the site of the old Montgomery Prairie while Stoneham cemetery, just off 105, provides a resting place for many patriots of Texas history. Among them are Andrew and John Montgomery. Referencing a period in Andrew's life before he came to the later Stoneham area, a state marker in the Stoneham cemetery reads as follows:

> *Andrew Jackson Montgomery:*
>
> *Apr. 4,1801-Dec.3, 1863 Born in Blount County, Tennessee, Andrew Jackson Montgomery came to Texas in 1819 with the James Long Expedition. In 1823, as the first known settler in Montgomery County, he opened a trading post at the crossing of two Indian Trails. From his post emerged the town of Montgomery from which Montgomery County received its name. A veteran of the Battle of San Jacinto, Montgomery married Mary Mahulda Farris at age 43,and they had nine children.*

Selected Sources

Crittenden, George. "Crittenden Papers." Stoneham, Texas, 1960. Texas Center for Regional Studies Archives.

Eddins, Roy, and Old Settlers and Veterans Association of Falls County Texas. *History of Falls County, Texas*, 1947.

Grimes, Ben. "Ben Grimes Private Papers," n.d. Texas Center for Regional Studies Archives.

Jenkins, John. *The Papers of the Texas Revolution, 1835-1836*. Vol. 9. 10 vols. Presidial Press, 1973.

Kemp, L. W. "Grimes, Jesse." In *Handbook of Texas*, 3:342. Austin: Texas State Historical Association, 1996.

Montgomery, Andrew. Petition to Legislature 2/3 League of Labor Land Grimes County, Gwyn Morrison Notary Public Grimes County (1855).

Parker, James W., and Rachel Parker Plummer. *The Rachel Plummer Narrative: A Stirring Narrative of Adventure, Hardship and Privation in the Early Days of Texas, Depicting Struggles with the Indians and Other Adventures ...*, 1926.

Pierson, Edwin G. "Pierson, John Goodloe Warren." In *Handbook of Texas*, 5:197–198. Austin: Texas State Historical Association, 1996.

Wilbarger, John Wesley. *Indian Depredations in Texas: Reliable Accounts of Battles, Wars, Adventures, Forays, Murders, Massacres, Etc., Etc., Together with Biographical Sketches of Many of the Most Noted Indian Fighters and Frontiersmen of Texas*. The Steck Co., 1889.

CHAPTER EIGHT

Plantersville, Land of the Renaissance

The patriarch of the Montgomery's, William, father of John, Andrew and their siblings had a land grant adjoining those of Asa Yeoman's and John Landrum. Near the junction of these three grants a community developed. In 1853, three local planters each donated 10 acres of land to formalize a town. These were Judge Henry Griggs, Colonel Isaac Baker and Dr. Mitchell.

Texas Renaissance Festival

The biggest event related to Plantersville is the mammoth Texas Renaissance Festival. A few miles south of the town for eight weekends in October and November, crowds fill the highways to enjoy a unique day of adventure in the great park.

Saint Mary's Catholic Church

Another highlight is a visit to the historic Saint Mary's Catholic Church some two miles north of town. Built facing south along the Lower Coushatti Trace in 1894, the original church burned leading to a newer structure in 1917. It is truly a wonder to behold.

Joel Greenwood Cemetery

Directly across highway 1774 from the church and subject to a walk of a half-mile or so brings one to the site of the Old Joel Greenwood Cemetery. This is one of the most historic sites in original Montgomery County, for here are buried several figures of historic prominence in the area of the Cradle of Texas Road. One of these is J.G. W. Pierson, mentioned above. As already stated, among his numerous roles was de facto head of Robertson's Colony. It is believed that Pierson's wife, Elizabeth Montgomery, is also buried here although there is a marker with her name in Independence, a community Pierson helped begin. Also Elizabeth's father, William Montgomery, mentioned earlier, is buried here. William died shortly before Montgomery County was established.

Special Case of Owen Shannon

Another figure that looms large in the history of Montgomery County is Owen Shannon, a veteran of the US Revolutionary War, who is probably buried here. The reasoning centers on questions surrounding the death of his widow, Margaret Montgomery Shannon, in 1854. She was buried east of Joel Greenwood in the Jacob Shannon Evergreen Cemetery. The story was that due to the flooding of Big Dry Creek, she could not be buried by her husband. Later it was assumed that this was the present Lake Creek, which led to the supposition that Owen was buried east of Lake Creek in the town of Montgomery. However, Big

Dry was actually Cedar Creek, to the west of Margaret's burial place. This leads to the conclusion that Owen was buried, in 1834, among his wife's kinsmen at the Joel Greenwood Cemetery.

Jacob Shannon Evergreen Cemetery

The Jacob Shannon Evergreen Cemetery is some five miles east of Plantersville. To get there, stay on 105 until you come to Mt. Moriah Road on the north side. A turn here and a short drive and you are there. Jacob Shannon, who had an Indian Trading Post while playing a significant role in the affairs of Washington Municipality, was the son of Owen Shannon and Margaret Montgomery Shannon. Margaret is the inspiration for a significant chapter of the Daughters of the American Revolution, DAR.

Selected Sources

Crittenden, George. "Crittenden Papers." Stoneham, Texas, 1960. Texas Center for Regional Studies Archives.

Gandy, William Harley. *A History of Montgomery County, Texas,* 1952.

Montgomery, Robin. *The History of Montgomery County.* Jenkins Pub. Co., 1975.

CHAPTER NINE

Dobbin, and the Babe of the Alamo

Back to 105 and a few miles to the east brings one to the community of Dobbin. In 1878 the Central and Montgomery Rail Company ran a line through the future town site. This was part of the Navasota to Montgomery line. By the 1880s, erected at the site was a post office under the name of Bobbin. Quickly, Bobbin became a shipping point for lumber and cotton. Among the establishments of Bobbin were four sawmills and a gristmill. By 1909, a north-south line, the Trinity and Brazos Valley Railway, had intersected the town, giving rise to a name change for the community. Bobbin became Dobbin in honor of a railroad official.

"The Babe of the Alamo"

Just below Dobbin off FM 1486 is the Griffith place, a treasure from the past. Most notably, the family is associated with the Alamo's "messenger of defeat." Although he took no mercy on the fighters for freedom at the Alamo, General Santa Anna did allow Mrs. Susanna Dickenson, wife of an officer, with her fifteen-month-old daughter, Angelina, to leave; this was mainly to spread word of the Texan defeat of 6 March 1836. Even then, but for the intercession of Colonel Juan N. Almonte of the Mexican Army, it is questionable whether Santa Anna would have relented to their release. They did present Sam Houston with the word of the debacle; however, the results were positive in the sense that they provided the inspiration for the battle cry at the decisive victory at San Jacinto, "Remember the Alamo".

It was in later years, after these dramatic events, that a chapter in the story of Suzanna Dickenson's daughter, the "Babe of the Alamo", Angelina, was to center around the family of Noah Griffith, one of the first settlers of the original Montgomery County. Noah's son, John Meynard Griffith, married the Babe in 1851 and lived with her on the Griffith land just below Dobbin. Their home was across the road from the original site of Noah's homestead. The pastor who conducted the wedding ceremony was the noted Rufus Burleson, whom we will meet again in the chapter of Montgomery.

In his memoirs, Dr.Burleson said Angelina's mother persuaded her to marry Griffith. Burleson added that "I shuddered to see two such uncongenial spirits united ... When People marry where they do not love, they are apt to love where they have not married." After living with Griffith for three or four years and bearing him three children she drifted off to New Orleans, leaving her son, J. Meynard Griffith to be reared by his uncle Josh Griffith's family. Another son of John Meynard and the Babe, Dick, raised several children whom Angelina had by a latter marriage. (History of Montgomery County, 208-09)

Life was exciting for the Noah Griffith family. In 1832, on an occasion when Noah was away shopping for supplies at Harrisburg, he left his wife and young sons ranging in age from two to eleven years at home. While he was gone, a band of Indians camped near the house for several days. The mother, being frightened, nailed the shutters closed, allowing the summer heat to stifle the refugees in the house. In addition to this heat-induced misery, they suffered hunger due to a lack of supplies.

One day, in their desperate state, they were delighted to see two Sand Hill Cranes light in the yard near the door. Seizing the opportunity to save her family from starvation, Mrs. Griffith permitted Sercy, the oldest boy, to try to kill them for food. He shot one that is all the food they had until Noah returned from Harrisburg. The Indians never made any menacing signs, but the dramatic incident went down in the memories of the boys and their descendants (History of Montgomery County, 244).

Selected Sources

Burleson, Rufus Columbus, and Harry Haynes. *The Life and Writings of Rufus C. Burleson: Containing a Biography of Dr. Burleson by Harry Haynes; Funeral Occasion, with Sermons, Etc; Selected "Chapel Talks;" Dr. Burleson as a Preacher, with Selected Sermons*, 1901.

Montgomery, Robin. *The History of Montgomery County.* Jenkins Pub. Co., 1975.

PHOTOS OF
THE CRADLE OF
TEXAS ROAD

Washington on the Brazos. Photo, Joy Montgomery.

Anson Jones House, Barrington Farm. Photo Library of Congress, Prints & Photographs Division HABS TEX, 239-WASH, 1—2

Madisonville Cattleman's Association, Madisonville.
Photo courtesy Camilla Viator

Madison County Museum, Madisonville. Photo Camilla Viator

Woodbine Hotel opened in 1903 as the Shapiro
Hotel, Madisonville. Photo Camilla Viator

Annual Texas Mushroom Festival, Madisonville. Photo Camilla Viator

Bedias Indians Display "The Source" Sculpture
created by Monica A. Taylor and Lawrence T. Zink,
located in Huntsville, Texas. Photo Jim Evans.

Sarah Dodson Flag. Photo Joy Montgomery

Bedias Jail replica donated in Honor of McAdoo and Shorty
Plaster by their daughters Mackie Bobo, Nancy Cook,
and Meredith Manning. Photo by Joy Montgomery

Bedias, Texas Mural Creation by Kathy Harris. Photo Joy Montgomery

Official 2011 Jacob Austin Band picture. http://
www.jacob-austin.net/Photos.html

Old Oakland Cemetery. Photo Joy Montgomery

Anthony Kennard Home. Photo Library of Congress, Prints
& Photographs Division HABS TEX,93-ROPR,2–1

Red Top Cemetery. Photo by Joy Montgomery

Zuber photo by Joy Montgomery from Shiro Community Center

Historic Bridge, Anderson down park. Photo Robin Montgomery

Fanthorp Inn, Anderson, dating to 1834. Across the street from the gavesite of Kenneth Anderson, last vice president of Texas. Photo Joy Montgomery

Confederate Memorial Plaza, Anderson. Photo Joy Montgomery

Unique Grimes County Courthouse, Anderson,
Texas. Photo Joy Montgomery

Statue of Rene Robert Cavelier Sieur de La Salle in Navasota.
Gift from France, celebrating US Bicentennial. French cultural
attaché rededicated it, 5 May, 2012. Photo Robin Montgomery

Mance Lipscomb statue, Navasota. Photo Robin Montgomery

Noted artist Russell Cushman, and a model of his
larger statue of the famous marshall, Frank Hamer.
Photo Rosemary Smith, Navasota Examiner

Father and daughter, Leon Collins and Molly Bee, world-class folk artists of Navasota. Photo by Russell Cushman

Grimes Prairie and Jesse Grimes, namesake for Grimes County. Courtesy Ben Grimes

[4350]
[ROBINSON to PIERSON]

[To J. G. W. Pierson   February 13, 1836]
. . .It will be recalled that this district was surveyed by many of the
citizens of Montgomery and Grimes Prairie.
    Believing you are willing to serve your country in any way
that you can be useful and the alarming fact that the enemy force
commanded by Santa Anna in person is about to attack our beloved
country at all points and the unorganized and deplorable conditions
of the militia calls for prompt organization, I have therefore taken
the liberty to appoint you my aid-de-camp for the Municipality of
Viesca. You will make all the necessary purchases of supplies of
provisions, ammunitions, tents, pack horses for the men on their
march to Gonzales where you will gather men and officers and
report them to the officer in command. You are empowered to do
all things necessary for the defence of Texas for she must now fight,
submit or fly, and I hope everyone is ready to choose the first, and
if anyone wishes to serve Texas, let him do it now as others did at
San Antonio where they caused the Black Flag to come down and
the tyrant to implore for mercy. . . .
                                        [James W. Robinson

Montgomery Prairie. From Jenkins, *Papers of the Texas Revolution*

Saint Mary's Catholic Church, Plantersville. Photo Joy Montgomery

Jacob Shannon Evergreen Cemetery. Photo Joy Montgomery

Bust of Charles Stewart, designer of the Lone Star Flag,
at Conroe's Lone Star Monument and Flag Park, Stewart
made his home in Montgomery. Bust by noted Conroe
artist, Craig Campobella. Photo Joy Montgomery

Fernland Park, Montgomery. Photo Fernland Park.

"Montgomery County Walkway through time", seventy-foot mural spanning highway 105 as it traverses downtown Conroe. Chief artist, Mark C. Clapham. Photo courtesy Conroe CVB

Conroe's Mary McCoy, Texas Hall of Fame radio
personality and singer, with Elvis Presley, August 24,
1955. Photo courtesy Mary McCoy Coker

Lone Star Monument and Historical Flag Park. Photo Joy Montgomery

Roy Harris of Cut and Shoot Texas. Photo Harris Family.

Roy Harris, World class boxer of the late 1950s, whose fame
played the pivotal role in bringing a post office to Cut and
Shoot and later incorporation of the community. With Robin
Montgomery, Roy Harris is co-author of the book, *Roy
Harris of Cut and Shoot: Texas Backwoods Battler, 2012.*

Folk festivities in Deerwood, an Hispanic model
community. Photo courtesy of Maria Jordan.

Willis, city on the rise, proud of its world class notoriety of
the late 19th century, and its connection to Jack Johnson, first
African-American world heavyweight boxing champion.

Willis Railroad. Photo Willis, Texas website

Richard Williams gravestone, near New Waverly. Photo Larry Foerster

Henderson Yoakum House, Huntsville, Walker
County, TX. Photo from Library of Congress, Prints
& Photographs Division 236-HUNVI.V,1-

Sam Houston Statue, off I-45 near Huntsville,
Texas. Photo Joy Montgomery

Sam Houston Memorial Museum, Huntsville. Photo
courtesy of Sam Houston Memorial Museum

Dr. Robin Montgomery and Joy Montgomery, co-authors of
the Cradle of Texas Road book. Photo Dr. Ahia Shabaaz

CHAPTER TEN

Montgomery, Charles Stewart & the Lone Star Flag

At the intersection of 105 and FM149, the town of Montgomery became the county seat of the original Montgomery County on 1 March 1838. W.W. Shepperd, in July 1837, made the first known pitch for businesses to establish in the town. Montgomery was incorporated in 1848 with Judge Nat Hart Davis as the first mayor. In 1874, Willis successfully campaigned for an election to decide the site of the county seat, and actually defeated Montgomery by 788 to 646 votes. This was short, however, of the two-thirds majority necessary to declare victory. Montgomery, accordingly, continued to hold the seat of county government, even surviving a new election on 2 April 1880, by which it secured its place over Willis by a vote of 1308 to 1243. Alas, in 1889, the new town of Conroe defeated Montgomery by 62 votes to assume the title of county seat.

Yet Montgomery continues to play a vital role in the county, both in commerce and in capitalizing upon its storied past. Entering the town from the north one is greeted by a state marker erected in 1936 recognizing W. W. Shepperd's advertisement in the *Telegraph and Texas Register* in July 1837 offering lots for sale. Also listed on the marker are the commissioners officially designated to search for a suitable site for the county seat:

> TOWN OF MONTGOMERY:
>
> *Founded in July, 1837 by W. W. Shepherd [Shepperd]-Incorporated in 1848-Montgomery County was created December 14, 1837 James Mitchell, Pleasant Gray, William Robinson, Elijah Collard, Charles Barnett, Joseph L. Bennett, Dr. B.B. Goodrich, D.D. Dunham and Henry Fanthorp, Commissioners, Selected Montgomery as the county seat and it remained as such until 1889 — Important trade center before the civil war.*

Charles Bellinger Stewart

Montgomery was the home of Dr. Charles Bellinger Stewart, Texas's first secretary of state, signer of the Texas Declaration of Independence, a state representative and the officially designated designer of the Lone Star Flag.

Charles B. Stewart was born on 6 February 1806 in Charleston, South Carolina. By the time his body received internment in the cemetery of Montgomery in July of 1885, the saga of Charles Stewart reached across the political spectrum of his adopted state. Arriving in Texas in 1830, Stewart immediately had an impact on events, serving, for instance, at the critical Battle of Velasco in 1832. But the contributions of Charles Stewart to the Texas cause would resonate not only on the battlefield. Among his many accomplishments in the political realm in aiding the cause of Texas's preparation for winning its independence was service as secretary of two governments of the Texans.

The first serious effort of the Texans to form a government of independence went by the name of the Permanent Council. Under Richard Royall, the president of that council, Charles Stewart served as secretary. Then under the successor entity to the Permanent Council, known as the Provisional Council, Stewart once again became the secretary. It was this that made him, effectively, the first Texas Secretary of State.

The permanent council yielded its authority to the "Consultation of the Chosen Delegates of All of Texas, in General Convention Assembled" on 3 November 1835. The fundamental question that the delegates from the municipalities of the departments of Brazos and Nacogdoches had to resolve was, for what were they fighting? After much deliberation, the assemblage decided that the goal of the troops in the field was to restore the Mexican Constitution of 1824, which had established a federal system of government.

With the purpose of the fighting thus determined, the consultation proceeded to give its official endorsement to most of the work of the permanent council, to adopt a plan for the organization of a provisional government.

That government comprised a governor, Henry Smith, and a lieutenant governor, James W. Robinson. Henry Smith appointed Charles Stewart as his Executive Secretary, an office at that critical period of the State's history, second only in importance to that of governor. In this position, Stewart rendered signal service to the government. He was methodical, courteous and affable, and the records of his office were kept in complete order. "When the Chief Executive or the General Council desired to examine any particular file of his office, he was always ready to put his hands on it without a moment's delay."

The most unfortunate part of the provisions of the council was the lack of a clear delineation of power between the governor and the governing council. This fact soon proved to be the undoing of the provisional council. After the adjournment of the consultation on 14 November, the council and the governor drew so far apart on the issue of the correct war policy that by 17 January, a complete stalemate had occurred. After that date the only effective semblance of a provisional government before March was an advisory committee that worked with Lieutenant Governor Robinson.

Throughout the crisis Charles Stewart remained steadfast in his support of Governor Smith. Stewart's refusal to turn over the archives of his office to Lieutenant-Governor Robinson, who the council had recognized as governor, caused Stewart to be fined $2,500. However the council did not make a serious effort to collect. (*History of Montgomery County, p197-99*)

Governor Smith appreciated Stewart's steadfastness to his cause as is seen in the following statement (*Signers of Texas Declaration of Independence, 239*):

> *Mr. Stewart was very conscientious and scrupulously honest in all his dealings, both of a private and public nature. He was not easily disturbed by adverse criticism, and when the General Council demanded that the records of his office be turned over to them, he refused without displaying anger or concern. When they attempted to discharge him for refusing to obey their demands, he continued to perform his duties as if nothing had occurred, merely informing me of these happenings without comment.*

Upon completing his term at the position of secretary, Charles Stewart received election to membership in the Convention of Washington-on-the-Brazos where, on 2 March 1836, he became a signer of the Texas Declaration of Independence. He went on to represent Montgomery County at the Constitutional Convention of 1845 and in the First, Fourth and Fourteenth legislatures.

Meanwhile, Mr. Stewart served as a medical doctor and

pharmacist, professions that he pursued upon moving to the town of Montgomery by 1837. But the activity of Charles Stewart, which most endears him to citizens of Montgomery County, and its friends along the extended Cradle Road, occurred in 1839. That was the year he served on a special committee of the Third Congress of the Republic of Texas charged with the duty of designing a new state flag.

Below are words from a state marker in Montgomery acclaiming the life of Charles B. Stewart:

> *Charles Bellinger Stewart:*
>
> *(1806-1885) First Secretary of State in Texas (Nov.1835-Feb.1836). Came to Texas 1830. Signed Declaration of independence; helped to write Constitution of the Republic in 1836 and the state in1845; served Montgomery County as district attorney and three terms as State Representative. Highest appointed official in Texas, keeper of the state seal, the secretary of state is named by the governor with advice and consent of the Senate. This office has attracted leaders. Stephen F. Austin, Father of Texas, held the post in 1836. Secretary Ebenezer Allen in 1845 represented the Republic in annexation, reserving for Texas her public lands—a prerogative allowed to no other state. The secretary of state grants charters; attests the commissions and proclamations of the governor; assists the governor to the many state boards, administers the uniform commercial code of Texas; appoints notaries, publishes the laws of Texas; administers election laws; issues ballots; canvasses returns; files reports of state agencies. Since Stewart, 83 other men and two women have served Texas as secretary of state.*

On the 30th of May 1997, Texas Governor George W. Bush signed House Resolution 1123 recognizing Montgomery County as the birthplace of the Lone Star Flag of Texas. The resolution stated in part "Dr. Charles Stewart of Montgomery County created this inspirational banner." An inspiration to us all, Dr. Charles B. Stewart reigns tall in the annals of Texas and a figure extraordinary along the Cradle of Texas Road.

Lesson of the "Nigh Cut"

An experience portraying the conditions and flavor of the culture of old Montgomery may be captured with the experience of Dr. Rufus Burleson (the same Dr. Burleson whom we saw in the chapter on Dobbin, with the "Babe of the Alamo"). He was at the time a pastor in Houston and was scheduled to preach the introductory sermon before the Union Baptist Association that met at Huntsville. The second morning of his journey found him in Montgomery, still lacking close to twenty-five miles. Upon learning that a Baptist lady had recently settled there, he decided it worth a small delay to see her. Baptists being so scarce, only 1,900 in Texas, Burleson was delighted to find her an elegant Christian lady from Tuscaloosa, Alabama the wife of Colonel Aaron Shannon, a wealthy farmer.

Mrs. Shannon likewise was delighted to see him, and was longing to have regular preaching and a church organized in Montgomery. Soon she said, "Brother Burleson, there is another Baptist lady, Mrs. Dr. Arnold, just settled in Montgomery from Providence, Rhode Island, and she is so anxious to see a Baptist preacher, I will send over for her and she will come and we will all be together." Burleson replied that he would be delighted to see her; however, he needed to be on his journey for he had "been told that I must get through the Big Thicket and San Jacinto bottom before dark, or I will be swamped."

In spite of his protestations, Burleson was persuaded to stay for dinner and even to remain afterward explaining "some things in the Bible, about foreknowledge and predestination." Finally convincing his hostesses of the wisdom of his rapid departure, they kindly replied,

"Brother Burleson, if you will take a nigh cut through the Big Thicket, you can save six miles; the people on horseback often take that nigh cut, rather than go the wagon road which is six miles further."

It happened that the ladies were unaware of the numerous trees, which now pervaded the road due to a tornado. These conditions, in concert with the darkness, conspired to test the preacher's faith. At first he spurred his trusty horse through the dimly lighted and narrow trail with measured success, but before he reached the San Jacinto bottom, his horse grew wearier and the darkness grew heavier. He found himself increasingly attempting to guide his steed out of briar patches and back on to the path. Finally he said to himself, "If I wander away from the road in this dense thicket, I may not be able to find my way back at all, so I will stop and rest till the moon rises, which I knew would be about 11 o'clock that night."

While thus reflecting on the folly of taking the nigh cut, he heard first a few and later an ever increasing number of wolf howls. Thoughts ran through the mind of the preacher, ranging from Daniel in the lion's den to Paul when he fought with the wild beasts at Ephesus. After praying and watching for some time he began to sing to give himself courage, but he apparently calmed the beasts through his singing. At the rise of the moon, he guided his mount gingerly along the narrow dim trail, to the beat of religious hymns interspersed with Hallelujahs from the wolf chorus stalking him on either side. Great was his relief when he crossed the San Jacinto and at last beheld the distant light of a settler's cabin.

Burleson stated that the lesson he learned that night was remembered for fifty years and often used in his lectures to the young in Sabbath Schools and chapel services: "to beware of taking nigh cuts and especially of letting anybody on earth, male or female, saint or sinner, persuade you to do wrong, and then tell you to take a nigh cut."(*History of Montgomery County, p154-56*)

Fernland

Evidence of the historic mindset of the citizens of Montgomery, located next to the Charles B. Stewart Library on Bessie Price Owen Street is Fernland Historical Park and Museum and Memory Park. Fernland is composed of a number of historic homes that have been relocated to the City using volunteers, donations and "Four B Funds." These are funds resulting from a requirement of the State of Texas for cities like Montgomery to set aside a portion of their sales tax revenues (4b) for the enhancement of business, tourism and the quality of life of its residents. Fernland is a joint venture between Fernland Inc., Montgomery and Sam Houston State University. Memory Park is operated under the direction of the Lake Conroe Rotary Club.

Fernland is a 40-acre parcel of land donated to Sam Houston State University in 2002. Carroll and Mae Tharp acquired the first of five historic buildings from Montgomery and Walker Counties in 1974. They painstakingly dismantled the structures before moving them to the original Fernland, from where they were restored before finding their way to Montgomery. The most famous structure on the site is Bear Bend, a hunting lodge that Sam Houston frequented.

Brenda Beavens, Billy Ray Duncan and the Montgomery Historical Society

Playing a key role in promoting Fernland and the general history and culture of Montgomery is the *Montgomery Historical Society*. Among the dynamic individuals of the group are Billy Ray Duncan and Brenda Beavens. Brenda is a history teacher whose work with kids is legendary across a broad swath of the Cradle of Texas Road. Perhaps she is most famous for the historical scavenger hunts she promotes, which sets her students to researching over a wide area.

Harley Gandy, Montgomery County Legend

The scholar who set the standard for research on Montgomery County history was Harley Gandy. Beginning with his famous master's degree thesis in 1952 at the University of Houston, over the years his influence continued in various forums, including as a popular public school teacher and principal. Mandatory to any study of Montgomery County history is to begin with a review of Harley's work as the base of the study.

Selected Sources

Burleson, Rufus Columbus, and Harry Haynes. *The Life and Writings of Rufus C. Burleson: Containing a Biography of Dr. Burleson by Harry Haynes; Funeral Occasion, with Sermons, Etc; Selected "Chapel Talks;" Dr. Burleson as a Preacher, with Selected Sermons*, 1901.

Kemp, Louis Wiltz. *The Signers of the Texas Declaration of Independence*. The Anson Jones press, 1944.

Montgomery, Robin. *The History of Montgomery County*. Jenkins Pub. Co., 1975.

CHAPTER ELEVEN

Conroe, Budding
Multicultural Center

Lone Star College-Montgomery

Though a new town by terms of the battles for Texas's Independence, Conroe, some fifteen miles east of Montgomery on 105, is proud of the heritage of Texas permeating its area. Reflective of this pride is the Lone Star College-Montgomery, a pivotal part of the Lone Star College System. The greater Lone Star system comprises the largest institution of higher education in the Houston area and the fastest growing community college system in Texas.

Presiding over the Conroe branch of the Lone Star network is the president, Dr. Austin Lane. Dr. Lane's innovative and progressive outlook epitomizes the community of Conroe, as seen in its plethora of visionaries.

Mark C. Clapham

Just one of those many visionaries was the late Mark C. Clapham. His awesome seventy-foot mural entitled "Montgomery County Walkway through time" spans 105 as the highway traverses down town Conroe. Winner of multiple awards, Mark was most proud of his Native American heritage, through his mother, a Chickasaw. Several of his paintings depict the impact of Native Americans on American history and the impact of history on the Native Americans. Truly an artist extraordinary and a marvelous human being was Mark Clapham.

Craig Campobella

Another cultural icon of Conroe is the visionary artist, Craig Campobella. His latest achievement lies in the one of a kind flag park just outside the main Montgomery County Library. The park features thirteen flags significant to the independence of Texas. The flags, in turn, surround Campobella's masterpiece, a fourteen-foot statue called "The Texian." The flag park, which also features a bust of Charles Stewart by Campobella, is in the process of expansion with plans that would make Conroe one of the primer cultural centers of the nation.

Dave Parsons

As a further honor to Craig Campobella, Dave Parsons wrote a marvelous poem about Craig's statue, The Texian. This is especially significant given that Parsons, a creative writing instructor at Lone Star College-Montgomery in Conroe, in 2011 received the Texas Commission on the Arts award as the Poet Laureate of Texas.

Mary McCoy

Not only in the arts, but in music, Conroe is blessed. In 2010, country artist, Mary McCoy, received induction into the Texas Radio Hall of Fame. At the time of the induction, her career spanned 59 years and included performances with Elvis Presley, among numerous other stars. To celebrate, Conroe Mayor Webb Melder issued a proclamation celebrating "Mary McCoy Day" in Conroe.

Isaac Conroe

In 1881, Houston lumberman and former captain in the Union Army, Isaac Conroe, established a sawmill two miles east of the International and Great Northern Railroad line. Conroe ran a tramline to the railroad, and then soon established a new mill off the tracks. The location became a station on the IGN and in 1884 a post office, which took the name of Conroe's Switch. With the Gulf, Colorado and Santa Fe Line crossing the IGN at Conroe's Switch, the community became a center for the budding lumber business. Dropping the word Switch from its name, Conroe quickly rose to succeed Montgomery as the location of the county seat.

A state marker to the town of Conroe records the essence of the history of the community:

Established in the forest in 1881 as Isaac Conroe's sawmill, 2 and one-half mi. east of present site, at juncture of two railroads, first named Conroe's Switch; then Conroe's; in 1890,Conroe. Lumbering brought prosperity. Chosen county seat in 1889. The country was still so wild, a deer was shot on the Square during Courthouse construction. Incorporated, 1904. Continued to grow in spite of several epidemics, two disastrous fires. The 1931 Strake Oil discovery turned it into a boom town. Now an industrial, forestry and petroleum center. Incise in base; Montgomery County Historical Survey Committee, 1966.

George W. Strake

The Strake oil discovery mentioned in the marker references George W. Strake, the man responsible for Conroe's appellation of "The Miracle City." Should one have been around the Conroe area in the nineteen twenties and early thirties one would wonder where the miracle was. At that time, reflective of the national scene during the Great Depression, pessimism in Conroe reined. The once thriving timber industry was evidencing a steep decline, forcing the closure of many mills. in 1930, a major Conroe bank failed, generating financial doldrums across the land. Conroe's schools struggled to complete their terms.

However, by 1933, the Conroe area was experiencing a precipitous rise in its fortunes. The Conroe school district became one of the State's wealthiest and for a brief time Conroe claimed more millionaires per capita than any other town in the United States. This was because George W. Strake knew what he was about and he never gave up, never allowed circumstances to get the best of him. Strake was born in St. Louis in 1884. Upon graduating from St. Louis University in 1917, he served in the US Army Corps of Engineers in World War I. On completing his tour of duty, he amassed a small fortune in Mexico then immediately lost it in Cuba.

George Strake, however, was not deterred. He proceeded to set up a base of operations in Houston from where he leased some 8,500 acres of land southeast of Conroe. Everything seemingly was working against him; many dry holes followed and the experts opined that no oil was to be found in the area. Meanwhile, a respectable oil field was under development west of Conroe. Only Strake had faith in the east.

So what did George W. Strake do? He hocked his belongs and continued his quest. Finally he met success. Did he ever! After an initial modicum of success in late 1931, on 5 June 1932 he struck black gold at 5,026 feet. Quickly, the resultant Conroe Oil Field became the third largest in the United States. Thus did the boomtown of Conroe receive the title of "Miracle City".

George Strake did not forget from whence came his strength. He was a strong Christian man of the Catholic faith. Among his honors were two of the Vatican's highest for a layman—the Order of Sylvester and the Order of Malta. In 1937, Strake represented the governor and the state of Texas at the United States presidential inauguration. Part of Strake's great legacy is Camp Strake just south of Conroe, among the nation's premier scout camps.

On 5 June 1957, the twenty-fifth anniversary of his great oil strike, Conroe honored its benefactor. Governor Price Daniel issued a proclamation designating this George Strake Day in Montgomery County. On 6 August 1969, this progenitor of the Miracle City went to meet the God he revered. (*Historic Montgomery County, 28-30*)

Following is a state marker to the *Conroe Oil Field*:

One of the great petroleum areas of the Texas coastal region. Opened Dec.13, 1931, by the discovery well of George Strake (No.1 South Texas Development Co.), about 1.4 miles west of here. Initial daily flow: 15,000,000 cubic feet of gas, along with white gasoline. Strake's second well, a 900-barrel-a-day producer, and the Heep Oil Corp. No.1 Freeman (both coming in during June 1932) proved existence of a large field. Fast-paced drilling ensued. In Jan.1933 Madeley No. 1, of Kansas Standard, came in as a wild well and on fire. TNT charges and tons of earth did not smother the fire, it burned about three months. Cratering spread to Harrison and Abercrombie well nearby, and that gushed out of control. In Jan. 1934 a driller for Humble killed the blowout, by using directional drilling for first time in coastal Texas. This saved the field. (The crater is 600 feet deep.) The Conroe field was the first in Texas to adopt 20-acre spacing, before this was mandatory under conservation rules. It has yielded over 400,000,000 barrels of oil; now produces at the yearly rate of 5,300,000 barrels. After the dramatic discovery here, Montgomery County developed 11 other oil fields, and has vast reserves for continuing production.

Conroe Normal and Industrial College

Another great Conroe visionary made his mark in education. During the early years of post-Civil War Texas, segregation cast a pale over efforts of African-Americans to be educated. In those few schools for African-Americans in existence, most of the teachers were white Christians. At the beginning of the twentieth century, only one major university for African-Americans existed, Prairie View A&M. Seeking, at that time, to enhance the educational capacities of African-Americans was an enterprising individual named Dr. Jimmie Johnson. The place he chose to reveal his great vision was Conroe. Dr. Johnson and his wife, Chaney, labored mightily to raise funds for their chosen work. At last, in April 1903, they met success. Conroe Normal and Industrial College was ready for service. For three hard years, Dr. Johnson and Chaney taught, worked and built on their creation.

An indication of the success of the Johnsons may be gleaned from an article published in the *Palestine Daily Herald* on 1 April 1905, under the title, "A Worthy Institution." The article states that J. B. Rayner, a representative of the Conroe College, was in Palestine, Texas soliciting funds for the educational institution. The funds were to "help erect a hall of Faithfulness on the campus." The faithfulness referenced was that of African-American slaves to the American dream, even during the Civil War. Students were to "secure their peace and material prosperity" through pursuing that long-cherished dream of a common culture of prosperity.

The reporter of the Palestine paper opined, "With this lesson well learned, and put into practice, there would be no race question to disturb the south." The reporter also noted "The Conroe school has already attracted the attention of our best and most thoughtful people, not only in the state, but throughout the country."

Quoting J. B. Rayner, the article categorizes as follows the lessons for students of Conroe Normal and Industrial College: "The science and art of politeness [Obedience] to law and respect for public sentiment. How to resist temptation and be virtuous ... idleness is sin—all labor is honorable ... A good character is the greatest wealth ... Christianity means love and service."

In 1906, exhausted from his noble and pioneering efforts, Dr. Johnson sold his college to the Baptist District Association, which association appointed to the presidency, Dr. David Abner.

Dr. Abner was a brilliant choice. For starters, he was the first graduate of Bishop College, a school started in Marshall, Texas in 1881 under the auspices of the American Baptist Home Mission Society. Unhappy that Bishop College was established in East Texas in 1884 the Guadalupe Baptist Association founded Guadalupe College in Seguin. Dr. Abner, the Bishop graduate, helped ease the tension between these two schools when he assumed the presidency of Guadalupe College. He left the latter position to assume the reigns of administration at Conroe Normal and Industrial College. Hence, he brought with him students and personnel from both east and west central Texas.

In 1919, succeeding Dr. Abner to the presidency was University of Chicago educated, Dr. William Johnson, who served until 1946. Drs. Abner and Johnson tenures saw to rebuilding the infrastructure and enhancing the curriculum offerings at the Conroe College. The most magnificent building unfortunately burned, a five-story structure housing female students.

During these depression and World War-plagued years, students were obedient and disciplined. For example, all were expected to work, boys largely in the field at such tasks as tending hogs and growing vegetables, while the young ladies worked inside. And the girls were required to wear black skirts and white middy blouses to classes, while the boys wore formal attire, coat and tie.

The last major building to grace the land of Conroe Normal and Industrial College, along Tenth Street, was the majestic Calhoun Edwards building erected during the tenure of acting president, The Reverend J. S. Curry, 1963-67. Though now abandoned, boarded up, the building yet stands majestic. Echoing its storied past, the marquee in front yet reads in bold letters, "Conroe College –Welcome American Baptist Convention of Texas."

And still gracing the front lawn, atop a pillar of white and exquisite stone, is a golden bell, reflective of the golden past that will always mark the spirit of enterprise and adventure that was Conroe Normal and Industrial College. *(Courier Column, Robin Montgomery)*

Rita Wiltz, Children's Books on Wheels, CBOW

Possessed of the same spirit of African-American determination as the leaders of Conroe Normal and Industrial College is Rita Wiltz. Descendent of pioneers of the unincorporated community of Tamina eight miles south of Conroe, Rita has the heart, courage and energy to motivate underprivileged youth.

Her vehicle is her non-profit organization, Children's Books on Wheels. Where children cannot afford books or the way to obtain them, there is Rita and her volunteers. Her goal is to promote literacy, in all its various forms. These include after school tutoring, math games, educational support, storytelling activities, and cultural arts events. Her target population is pre-K to 12th grade students. Her program of providing books for underdeveloped rural communities includes over 300 children serving both Montgomery and Walker Counties. The organization furthermore provides referral and resources for the Texas

Health and Human Services Association applications and brochures for CHIP Children's Medicaid, CHIP Prenatal, Food Stamps, and Texas Women's Programs. High School job workshops and summer outreach programs are an important component of Children's Books on Wheels as is information on preventing HIV/AIDS and STD's, substance abuse, and Teen Self-Esteem trainings.

In the spring of 2012, CBOW received a proclamation from the office of Houston Mayor, Annise D. Parker. Also a certificate of appreciation at the Federal Reserve Bank of Houston was awarded for the group's "commitment to financial education of individuals and families" through its partnership with Houston Money Week 2012.

CBOW maintains the library at Tamina Community Park.

Marlen Tejeda

As with African-Americans, Conroe is blessed with enterprising and visionary Hispanics. In recent times, Conroe is becoming the center of a growing Hispanic presence. One of the most energetic and empathetic of this community is Marlen Tejeda. Marlen is an educator, independent educational consultant and social change facilitator. She coordinates free adult educational programs with 300 adult students attending night classes. Among the subjects taught are English as a second language, elementary, secondary and GED classes at the Hispanic Task Force Plaza Comunitarias and citizenship classes at no cost to participants in Conroe.

Through the creation and promotion of diverse programs related to the Hispanic Community, Marlen has contributed to an upwardly mobile perspective on the part of Latin American migrants to Conroe. Furthermore, she has contributed to enhancing the work place of day laborers and farm workers. Among yet other engagements, Marlen is the founder and president of Latin Friends of Conroe, vice-president of the Conroe Latin American-Chamber of Commerce and volunteer for the Mexican Consulate.

Besides all these noble endeavors, Marlen is also an advocate for women's rights, engaging issues of gender equality, supporter of battered women's groups and participant in medical campaigns for cancer prevention, social assistance for the terminally ill, and even with repatriation of cadavers.

Marisa Olivares Rummell

The Conroe area is truly blessed, for Marlen is not the only visionary among its ever-expanding Hispanic community. Among those many is Marisa Olivares Rummell. She is the successful business owner of three manufacturing companies: one in California and two in Texas. She is the first chairperson and on the founding board of the Montgomery County Hispanic Chamber. She was even honored with a White House Appointment and is an advisor to Congress on Hispanic issues.

Alejandra Tapia

A former educator at the Universidad Nacional Autónoma de Mexico, Alejandra Tapia has added much to the culture of Conroe and the area of the Cradle Road. Among her innovations, she has raised awareness of the influence of the ancient culture of the Aztecs of Mexico on the culture of Texas. Her "Chikawa Aztec Dance and Traditions" is a group that explores the cultural aspect of Mesoamerican roots. Chikawa means strong in the Nahuatl language. The Conroe-based organization is a mixture of children and adults. Chikawa also supports the conservation education of diverse groups and organizations while Alejandra has furthermore worked as a high school completion specialist for the Conroe Independent School District. She is fluent in the Nahuatl language in addition to French, Spanish and English.

Alejandra Tapia, Marisa Rummell, Marlen Tejeda and so many more specialists in broadening cultural awareness, make the future bright for a viable and stable culture along the Cradle of Texas Road.

Conroe Celebrations

In October, Conroe citizens are treated to two major events of fun, food and celebration. One, a Lobster Fest, is under the sponsorship of the Greater Conroe Lake Conroe Chamber of Commerce. The other is a Catfish Festival, orchestrated by the "Friends of Conroe."

In April other exciting events are on the docket. For example, "Conroe Live", a non-profit, celebrates the history behind Conroe's downtown buildings. Then there is the Montgomery County Fair at the Fair Grounds. It is also in April, that the magnificent Flag Park has its annual lowering and raising of its 13 flags symbolic of Texas history. Meanwhile, the Crighton and Owen Theaters are never devoid of classic and front-line entertainment of various genres.

Selected Sources

Foerster, Larry. "Private Collections and Correspondence," 2012.

Montgomery, Robin. *Historic Montgomery County: An Illustrated History of Montgomery County, Texas.* Historical Pub. Network, 2003.

—————. "Newspaper Coloumns from Conroe Courier and on Texas Center for Regional Studies Website," n.d.

Various. "Websites: Marlen Tajeda, Marisa Olvares Rummell, Chikawa, and Rita Wiltz," n.d.

CHAPTER TWELVE

Cut and Shoot, Roy Harris: World-Class Boxer and Citizen

C ut and Shoot Texas is a fabled community off 105, six miles east of Conroe. It is more than just a town of world renown. It is a state of mind reflective of a readiness to fight for one's beliefs while respecting a reasonable compromise. Let's explore how this unique community received its name and later its world fame.

Naming of Cut and Shoot:

Our story begins in July 1912. One would presume it was hot. The center of the community was a building called the "Community House," a combination church and school. Certain religious denominations, however, were excluded from using the facilities. Then it happened: 21 July 1912 marked the day that an evangelist of one of the excluded groups scheduled an appearance, bent on conducting a service. Opposing factions emerged and on that July morning, they met, each with weapons concealed but within reach. One side was determined to enter the building to have a preaching. The other side was just as determined to prevent said preaching.

As tension mounted, Jack King, an eight-year-old of one of the families in favor of having the preaching, became frightened. Consequently seeking to do something, it is said that he blurted out, "I'm going to cut around the corner and shoot through the bushes." Fortunately, no cutting and shooting occurred on that day courtesy of a compromise solution. The visiting evangelist was allowed to engage a series of meetings over the next several weeks. Instead of the church, though, his platform was a shaded spot on the ground while the congregation was composed of families seated in their nearby wagons.

Meanwhile, trials were set for the leaders of the respective feuding factions. At one of the gatherings, a witness named Archie Vick was asked where the confrontation had occurred. Since the place did not have a name, Vick responded that it was "where they had the cutting and shooting scrape." Shortened to "Cut and Shoot," the name stuck. (Gandy, A History of Montgomery County)

Roy Harris

Though the community had long since received its name, it did not receive a post office until 18 August 1958. The story behind this event is one of the most colorful of the stories along the Cradle Road. In 1958, Roy Harris of Cut and Shoot was the third-ranked heavyweight boxer in the world. It was on 18 August 1958, with the world's heavyweight boxing championship on the line, that Roy met Floyd Patterson, former Olympic gold medal winner and reigning world champion. Much to Roy's chagrin, the referee stopped the fight after twelve rounds because Roy had sustained a cut.

But Roy Harris had captured the heart of the nation and of the world and he had made a little burg east of Conroe, about which few outside its environs had ever heard, a household name. On Decca, a major record label, Roy even recorded a song about the town. Called "Cut 'n Shoot, Texas, USA", the song set many a hand to clapping and enticed visitors by the scores to visit the place. Literally, Roy put Cut and Shoot on the map, as the post office emerged due to his fame.

In the forest of Cut and Shoot, Roy Harris had enjoyed a colorful youth, raised among an amazing family. As a teenager, his brother, Tobe, also a boxer, landed with only a rope and a little boat, the largest alligator ever captured in Texas, over 14 feet long. Boxing fans were enthralled. As Roy began to rise in the rankings, a story about his life in Cut and Shoot for the *Fort Worth Star Telegram* received designation as sports story of the year in Texas. The author of the story became known thereafter as "Cut and Shoot Kellum."

But a major part of Roy's mystic was that he was more than just a great boxer. An honor student in college, Roy went on to teach 4th and 5th grades at Cut and Shoot elementary school before launching a successful career in real estate. In 1972, he earned a law degree, while in the process of holding the office of Montgomery County Clerk for seven consecutive terms. After 28 years he stepped down, never having tasted defeat as a politician. Along the way, with his beautiful wife, Jeannie, he raised a wonderful family of six children. (See *Roy Harris of Cut and Shoot: Texas Backwoods Battler*)

Debra Sue Maffet and Larry Butler

Other celebrities associated with Cut and Shoot include Debra Sue Maffet, Miss America, 1983 and Larry Butler, a country musician of Grand ole Opry Fame. Butler was once the mentor of famed country singer, Willie Nelson, when Willie was in his band.

Selected Sources

Gandy, William Harley. *A History of Montgomery County, Texas,* 1952.

Harris, Roy, and Robin Montgomery Dr. *Roy Harris of Cut and Shoot: Texas Backwoods Battler.* iUniverse, 2012.

Montgomery, Robin. *Cut'n Shoot, Texas: The Roy Harris Story.* Eakin Press, 1984.

———. *Historic Montgomery County: An Illustrated History of Montgomery County, Texas.* Historical Pub. Network, 2003.

CHAPTER THIRTEEN

Deerwood: Foundational Experiment in Cultural Integration

S till further to the east on 105 we come to Deerwood, a model community of some 350 Hispanics. While maintaining a unique feel for their native culture over three generations, the community is finding its place and engaging intercultural ties true to the *Tejano* experience. Since 2010, supporting this transition process has been a diverse team of professionals led currently by Maria Jordan and the Texas Latino Leadership Roundtable.

Deerwood emerged from the work of the Leatherwood family, who, around 1980 developed this property in a family friendly manner. Taking advantage, a handful of Latino families purchased lots, thus beginning a community. In 2004, residents organized a community center with a donated trailer and the help of Conroe Independent School Center social workers. Four years later, a team of resource professionals from around Montgomery County organized to form *Deerword Familia Project*. This helped residents identify their community priorities and begin connecting with outside resources.

Currently the village is about 90% Latino with the first generation of residents reaching retirement age and the first generation born in Deerwood entering the workforce and higher education. Deerwood remains unincorporated and feeds both Conroe and Splendora school districts. Many master craftsmen reside in this working class community while many small business owners also reside there. Surveys reveal that almost 70% of respondents have or wish to have their own business—including landscaping, bakers, seamstresses, chefs and masons. Deerwood has a strong bicultural identity holding onto mostly Mexican-American traditions and customs.

The study of the impact of those traditions and customs on Latinas (female Hispanics) and, in turn, of the impact of Latinas on society is a special role of the Texas Latino Leadership Roundtable. How this might impact in particular Conroe, one of the cities along the Cradle Road, may be depicted as follows:

According to the 2010 Census data, in Texas the growth rate of whites was 4.2 percent and blacks 22 percent. Meanwhile, the Hispanic population grew by 65 percent. In terms of percentage by race within the state, whites decreased from 52 percent to 45 percent, while Hispanics increased from 32 to 38 %. The emerging center of Hispanic impact in Texas is the Houston Metropolitan zone. In Montgomery County the rate of Hispanic increase was 155 percent. Most of the increase is concentrated in Conroe where whites are slightly less than 50 percent with Hispanics comprising about 40 percent of the population. We will look at some of the implications of these statistics, with emphasis on the important role of Latinas.

Central to those implications is the dropout rate in public schools. Nationally, it is projected that by 2018, only 28 percent of jobs will be available for non-high school graduates. Statewide in Texas, it is estimated that around 130,000 students drop out annually, leading to a nearly $400 million shortfall in state revenue via lost wages and taxes coupled with increases in Medicaid and social services. Here is where the Hispanic impact surfaces, for in Houston the dropout rate for Hispanics approaches 50 percent.

The Hispanic culture is traditionally family-centered with the woman holding the role of connector. This gives her wide influence over academic and other opportunities for her children. Many times, the first-generation Hispanic mother in the United States experiences difficulty in adjusting to problems of a new culture. The consequent lack of a viable role model in the new environment generates a special strain on second-generation Latinas, rendering them susceptible to a variety of mental health issues.

In the face of these difficulties, Latinas are showing a remarkable resilience. For instance, once introduced to the educational process, Latinas statistically do better than their male counterparts. Not only that, but in Texas where white men have a 42 percent college graduation rate, that of Hispanic women is 45 percent. Latinas also are having a growing impact in the business world with Latina-owned businesses generating some $55 billion annually. Addressing the obstacles before Latinas and enhancing the process of assimilating them into the larger culture is in the interest of us all.

The Texas Latino Leadership Roundtable, TLLR

Taking the lead in promoting awareness of the vital role of Latinas in general and of the Deerwood Community in particular is the Texas Latino Leadership Roundtable. The TLLR is a non-partisan, professional community organization established in 2010. The organization believes that strong communities need thoughtful, focused, and local support for great success. The vision centers on helping to prepare the Hispanic community for social, economic and civic integration into the larger general culture in a manner beneficial to all.

Maria Baños Jordan is the Executive Director and co-founder of TLLR with Mario Rosales and other active Latino professionals from the community. With a BA in sociology from the University of Houston, Maria has focused her efforts for eighteen years on Latino family support. She has developed several successful outreach efforts in Montgomery County since 2008. Among these are the Hispanic Outreach Professional Enrichment program and the Conroe Historias Project and Biography Compilation archived in Montgomery County Libraries. These efforts have helped raise awareness of a growing ethnic population.

Maria believes "Maestros/Teachers" can empower and guide through bicultural efforts. Her extensive range of activities include serving on the Montgomery County Emergency Assistance Board of Directors, Deerwood Familia Project Advisory Council, NALEO, DHS Houston Roundtable and contributing writer for *Familias Latinas* Magazine. Maria also is an active member of the Pan American Roundtable.

(*For a fuller look at Deerwood and the Texas Latino Leadership Roundtable see Cradle of Texas Road, Supplement, Three, a piece by Maria Jordan*)

The Pan American Roundtable

The Pan American Roundtable is a natural for Maria Jordan's interests, for it singles out the often overlooked and underestimated role of women in building bridges to cultural awareness and communication. The international organization stems from the vision of Mrs. Florence Terry Griswold. In 1916, a major revolution was boiling in Mexico. Mrs. Griswold realized how women could make a difference in spreading goodwill among nations by providing for refugees from the massive struggle going on south of the US border.

The motto of the PAR is "One for all and all for one," while the PAR symbol of the round table likewise signifies unity. High on the belief system of the organization is that only through education and communication, not legislation, can understanding and friendship grow. As this book goes to press, presiding over the local, Conroe, chapter of the Pan American Roundtable is Dr. Ahia Shabaz, an African-American former professor and current tireless worker for racial accord.

The Pan American Roundtable, the Texas Latino Leadership Roundtable and the citizens and associates of Deerwood Community, all are grand examples of building blocks to intercultural unity along the path of the Cradle of Texas Road.

Selected Sources

Jordan, Maria. "Maria Jordan, Director, Latino Leadership Roundtable," 2012. http://www.texaslatinoleadership.com.

————. "Texas Latino Leadership Roundtable," n.d. http://www. texaslatinoleadership.com.

Montgomery, Robin. "Conroe Courier," n.d.

Various. "Pan American Roundtable, Conroe," n.d.

CHAPTER FOURTEEN

Willis, Danville, Waverly, Memorable Triumvirate

B ack to Conroe and up Interstate 45 one soon comes to Willis. Greeting the visitor is the following marker that summarizes the town's great history:

Willis:

Founded in 1870.Named for P.J. and R.S. Willis (large land and timber owners who formerly were merchants in the area). They gave town site, on the Houston & Great Northern Railroad. With the line came prosperity, and in 1874 Willis and Montgomery vied for the county seat, but both eventually lost to Conroe. Willis boasted a college, opera house, numerous stores, and by 1895 had vast tobacco fields supporting 7 cigar factories. This industry faded when tariff on Cuban tobacco was lifted. Present industries are timber and livestock.

World-Class Tobacco Town

Notable is Willis's tobacco history in the 1890s, referenced in the marker. With politics limiting Cuba's dominance of the tobacco market, Willis capitalized, importing the finest grades and implanting them in its favorable soil. Tobacco from Willis received first prize at the World's Columbian Exposition in Chicago in 1893 and at Paris, France in 1900. One famous planter, William Spiller, lived comfortably in a sixteen-room mansion, which he christened *Esperanza*.

Difficulties in harvesting and taking the product to market began to limit the success of Willis tobacco. Then world trends brought Cuba once again into the place of dominance, ending Willis's time of basking in the world limelight.

Jack Johnson, first African-American Champion

One of Willis's most celebrated citizens, for a time intermittently in his youth, was Jack Johnson, who later became the first African-American to attain the world heavyweight boxing title. The story of his battles to embrace a segregated society is a classic tale of pathos.

The movie, the "Great White Hope", is based on the life this African-American. It was in 1908, one hundred years before an African-American would become president of the United States, that Jack Johnson became the world's heavyweight boxing champion. Though in that year he defeated Tommy Burns of Australia for the title, the title was disputed. Hence, Johnson had to wait until 1910 for his chance at boxing legitimacy. That chance came when former champion, Jim Jeffries, dubbed by writer Jack London, the "Great White Hope," came out of retirement to meet the challenge. Jeffries' loss to Johnson in what was billed the "Fight of the Century" led to race riots across the nation while a number of deaths ensued.

It was in this atmosphere of bitterness and racial strife that, in 1913, the testimony of a white woman of questionable reputation named Belle Schreiber led to Johnson's conviction under the Mann Act. Rather than succumb to an unjust jail sentence, John took his wife at the time, a white woman named Lucille Cameron, and spent the next seven years roaming the world. During this period, in 1915, he lost his heavyweight title to Jess Willard in Cuba. Finally, in 1920, Johnson returned to the United States, where he surrendered to a short jail sentence in Leavenworth, Kansas.

Upon his release, Jack Johnson engaged adventures in acting, music, exhibition boxing and other activities until a fatal car accident in 1946. Always controversial and outspoken, his legacy includes being the hero of the flamboyant heavyweight champion, Muhammad Ali, himself not a stranger to controversy. In 1954, Jack Johnson was admitted posthumously into the boxing Hall of Fame.

The amazing Jack Johnson was born in Galveston in 1878, one of six children whose father was a former slave who managed to fight for US forces in the Civil War. Although he and all of his siblings learned to read and write, Jack Johnson dropped out of school in the fifth grade. After that he roamed around Willis with his relative, "Tink" Golden. While in Willis, he engaged in numerous fights. Johnson also passed time in Montgomery with another relative named Bat Johnson. Fighting skills that he acquired during various sojourns in Montgomery County would serve him well in preparation for his clash with destiny on the world stage. (*Courier column, Robin Montgomery*)

Danville

A little north of Willis was once the thriving little community of Danville. To the area once came two brothers, Samuel and Joseph Lindley, who brought their families from Danville, Illinois around

1830, receiving Texas land grants in 1835. One of Samuel's sons, Jonathan, received immortality through his untimely death in the Alamo. For a while in the 1850s Dr. Charles Bellinger Stewart resided in the community that was by then called Danville, Texas.

On September 28, 1848, the *Telegraph and Texas Register*, under a heading entitled, "United States Mail," reported on a line of stagecoaches as follows: "this Line of Stages passes through the towns of Melrose, Nacogdoches, Douglass, Crockett, Cincinnati, Huntsville, Danville and Montgomery."

Chances are Sam Houston rode this line, for on 11 September 1858 in Danville he made one of most rousing speeches of his career. Over 500 people reportedly attended the event, a grand barbeque, which helped turn the gubernatorial tide for him in 1859.

About Sam Houston's speech The *Southern Intelligencer* of Austin reported the following on 29 September, 1858:

> *GEN. HOUSTON AT DANVILLE—A friend informs us that the speech of General Houston at Danville was of a different staple from the commodity of most of his efforts. He dealt in no personalities, but only upon political topics. He condemned Yankee and the Southern Leaguers, and denied that it was possible for such a party to make headway in Texas. He expressed his devotion to the Union, the President, and the Administration. Our informant, an old Democrat, says it was the best effort of the General's life, and promises us a further report of the speech.*
>
> *We shall be very glad to hear that the General has renounced his errors, and that, forgetting himself, he advocates the great principles, which oppose fanaticism at both ends of the Union.*
>
> *(See a fuller treatment of this speech and its implications, directly from sources of the time, in the supplementary section of this book—Supplement Four)*

An interesting piece featuring the merits of Danville is found in the *Texas State Gazette*, 24 May 1856:

> *This pleasant village is rapidly improving. It is situated in a central position between the towns of Montgomery, Huntsville, and Cold Springs.*
>
> *In the midst of a dense population of wealthy planters, who seem determined to make it what all country villages should be, a pleasant place of resort for the transactions of their neighborhood business, and for educational purposes. For some time good schools have been sustained there and recently the citizens have determined to erect a first rate educational edifice. The Baptists and Methodists both have church buildings in that place and have regular preaching. An interesting Sunday School on the Union plan, has for some time been sustained.*
>
> *Danville is in close proximity to the "Big Thicket" which is fast being settled and from whose citizens it deserves a considerable support. The citizens are quite industrious and temperate, which is evinced by the fact that the place does not contain a single grog shop. Danville is 65 miles from Houston which is its place of trade. Its merchants are enterprising business men and contribute largely to the commerce of Houston. One of them ranks among the wealthy men of the State. That gentleman is, also, quite a literary man and sometimes favors the public with the fruits of his researches and reflections, as the columns of the Telegraph will testify.*

Old Waverly

Another interesting side trip, just up I-45 from Danville, is the site of Old Waverly. The first major influx of settlers hailed from Montgomery, Alabama. These were slaveholders who used their servants to clear the land and build their homes. Many of the homes were built in the southern colonial style—long front galleries and big rooms with high ceilings. By the early eighteen fifties most of these homes had been completed and many literary conversations occurred within them. It was after one of these conversations that Colonel F. M. Lewis obtained a consensus to name the community Waverly after Sir Walter Scott's Waverly Novels.

Waverly soon became a flourishing community with a population of around 700 who gained a wide reputation as visionaries of finance, farming, education and culture. During this period the citizenry established an academy. The decline of Waverly emanated from the chaos wrought by the Civil War followed by the misfortune to have the railroad by-pass them.

Saga of Richard Williams

During reconstruction, the Yankees established a cavalry camp near Waverly that led to many legends, one of which concerned the house of a veteran of the Texas Revolution named Richard Williams. Apparently Williams mistook three federal soldiers who ventured too near his abode for Indians and shot them. Since Williams was a southerner and an old warrior, it is possible that he took advantage of an opportunity to do in some Yankees.

At any rate, legend has it that Williams buried the soldiers under his home and that their ghosts continue to haunt the place. It is possible that the soldiers and Williams are continuing their gun-battle in the spirit world as some stories have Williams himself playing the part of the ghost. *(History of Montgomery County, 263-64)*

(See Cradle of Texas Road Supplement Five, for a deeper look at Richard Williams, a work by Larry Foerster, of "Conroe Live")

Stately Elmwood Mansion

Union soldiers made another permanent impression on the area extending westward from Waverly when Cavalry Road became their namesake. The road originally extended from Waverly to Longstreet, an extinct town on the western fringes of present Montgomery County. Today, a cemetery marks the approximate site of another Union camp. Along this road a few miles west of present Willis was the northern entrance of the once stately southern manor of Elmwood, the plantation home of General A. J. Lewis. Elmwood was built by slaves brought over from Virginia and stands as one of the few frame houses in this section of the state.

These slaves labored for two years constructing the three-story mansion utilizing lumber from twenty sawmills. The bricks used on the house were imported from Holland and the house was put together with wooden pegs. In 1940 Elmwood was torn down so its lumber could be used in the construction of a new and modern dwelling.

Old timers in the area once said that before Elmwood's demise Lewis's carriage could be seen on moonlit nights meandering gracefully up the tree-strewn pathway to the stately veranda of Elwood House where magnificently clad ghostly figures would flitter through the picturesque doors to glide gracefully up the stair way to the majestically decorated ball-room on the third floor. The old timers swore that the shadows flickering in the moon light around that floor were caused not by trees but rather by the elite of the nineteenth century. (*History of* Montgomery *County, 264-65*)

New Waverly

The demise of Old Waverly came with its refusal to accept the railroad. Accordingly, in 1870, The Houston and Great Northern laid tracks ten miles to the west while setting aside a town site known initially as Waverly Station. As many residents of Old Waverly moved to the new site, soon the town took the name of New Waverly. In 1952 New Waverly incorporated as a "general-law" city.

Selected Sources

Foerster, Larry. "Short Biography of Richard Williams." In *Cradle of Texas Road*, Supplement Four. iUniverse, 2013.

Hailey, James. "New Waverly, TX." 4:1006. Austin: Texas State Historical Association, 1996.

Harris, Roy. "On Jack Johnson," n.d.

Montgomery, Robin. *Historic Montgomery County: An Illustrated History of Montgomery County, Texas*. Historical Pub. Network, 2003.

———. *The History of Montgomery County*. Jenkins Pub. Co., 1975.

CHAPTER FIFTEEN

Huntsville, Legacy of Sam Houston

Huntsville, a Major Educational Center

Up I-45 north from New Waverly, brings one to Huntsville, an educational hub of the Cradle of Texas Road. By 1844, in operation in Huntsville was the Huntsville Male and Female Academy. Also known as the Brick Academy, the school received its charter on 11 April 1846. Meanwhile, in the fall of 1845, Stovall's Male and Female Academy began operation. On 16 March 1848, the latter institution restricted its enrollment to males, becoming known appropriately enough as Huntsville Male Institute. Subsequently, the Brick Academy came to cater exclusively to females. In the early 1850s, the Methodist Church established Andrew Female College while Austin College also began offering courses in Huntsville.

Sam Houston: namesake of Sam Houston State University

Approaching Huntsville, one is greeted by a magnificent, world-class statue of Sam Houston, standing by the highway. Inside the city are two of Sam Houston's homes, plus his gravesite. A few miles out of town to the east is a marker to Raven Hill, site of yet another of Houston's homes.

As every student of Texas history knows, as a general, Houston led his troops to victory at the Battle of San Jacinto to secure independence for Texas. Then he twice served as president of the second Texas Republic and when Texas became a state served alternately as a United States Senator and governor. Before all of this, he was governor of Tennessee. It was in his honor that Sam Houston State University, founded in 1879, was named.

Especially important was the Old Main Building on Sam Houston Campus. Unfortunately the building, itself, no longer exists. This writer is one of those with fond memories of the most famous fixture on Sam Houston's campus, the dog, Tripod, who was allowed to sleep in Old Main, in general having the run of the place. The following marker stands on the site of Old Main:

> *Sam Houston State University- Old Main Building: First permanent structure built by state of Texas for teacher training—when Joseph Baldwin was president of Sam Houston Normal Institute. L.S. Ross was governor, and A.T. McKinney was chairman of the S.H.N.I. local board. Cornerstone was laid September 23, 1889, with main address by The Hon. O.M. Roberts, Governor when S.H.N.I. was chartered in 1879. Also present was state school superintendent Oscar H. Cooper, a member of the first faculty. Completed in 1891, Main gave institute its first library, 8 large classrooms, a distinctive chapel. Architect: Alfred Mueller.*

African-American Links to Sam Houston: Joshua Houston

Not only buildings, but also important people took Houston's name. Sam Houston's former slave, Joshua Houston, became a notable citizen in his own right. His is a remarkable story serving as a link between two remarkable men named Houston: his master, Sam Houston on the one hand, and his son, Samuel W. Houston on the other. After more detail on Joshua, himself, we will meet his son.

Joshua was raised as a slave on Temple Lea's plantation in Marion, Perry County, Alabama. At his death, Temple left Joshua and his family to his daughter, Margaret Lea, who took him to Texas in 1840 when she married Sam Houston. Joshua served the Houston's well, traveling often with Sam Houston and becoming a skilled blacksmith, wheelwright and stage driver. Against the grain of the times, The Houston's taught Joshua to read and write. The Houston's also allowed Joshua to work away from their property when Sam was out of town. Consequently, Joshua earned a respectable life savings of some $2000.00. Magnanimously, he offered these savings to Margaret Lea Houston upon Sam Houston's death, an offer she politely refused.

After the Civil War and the death of both Sam and Margaret Houston, Joshua Houston became a successful businessman, church leader and office holder. For instance, he received election as a county commissioner, alderman, a trustee of the first black church in Huntsville, the Union Church, and he promoted the establishment of Bishop College in Huntsville in 1883. In 1888, Joshua Houston was a member of the Texas delegation to the Republican National Convention. Joshua Houston was a slave who made the best of his situation, setting an example beyond his time. (*March to Destiny, 159-160*)

Samuel W. Houston

Joshua's son, Samuel W. Houston, was the namesake of a school for African-Americans some five miles west of Huntsville. The school was named Sam Houston Industrial and Training School. The following is taken from a marker to the school west of Huntsville off highway 30:

> Legislated after the close of the Civil War, the Texas Constitution of 1866 provided for a public school system supported by funds derived from property taxes; monies collected from African Americans would go to schools for their children. Although the law continued to change during the next decades, the primary providers of African American education were the Freedmen's Bureau, churches, missionary associations and philanthropists. Samuel W. Houston (1864-1945) was born in Huntsville to Joshua and Sylvester Houston. His father was a slave and personal bodyguard of former Texas President Sam Houston. His family believed strongly in education, and he earned degrees from the Hampton Institute in Virginia, Atlanta University in Georgia and Howard University in Washington, D.C. He returned to Huntsville in 1900 and established a newspaper. He then taught in Grimes County and at the Huntsville Community School before establishing a school circa 1906 near here in what was the Galilee community. The Sam Houston Industrial and Training School began in the Galilee Methodist Church, which Houston rented for the classes. He soon added teachers and programs, offering vocational curriculum as well as the arts and humanities. Trustees built the first schoolhouse in 1914 and continued to add facilities, including dormitories and workshops. By 1930, the school served hundreds of students from around the state. That year, the Sam Houston School merged into Huntsville colored school, which became Sam Houston High School. It closed

in 1968 due to integration. The foundation set by Houston and other early educators ensured the education of generations of African-American students in the 20th century.

Andrew Female College:

Another significant educational institution was Andrew Female College, as explained in the long marker quoted below:

> *Site of Andrew Female College: Andrew Female College was founded in 1852 and chartered in early 1853. It was named for Bishop James Osgood Andrew and sponsored by the Texas Conference of the Methodist Episcopal Church, although its charter allowed no religious tests for faculty or students. The Institutions first five-month session began in May 1853 in an old Huntsville College building, "The Brick Academy." At a time where there were few educational opportunities for women, enrollment was high and classes soon outgrew the academy. Citizens of Huntsville supported education for women by contributing funds for a larger, 2-story building completed in 1855. Eighty students, primarily from Walker and surrounding counties, were enrolled in the Andrew Female College in the 1856-1857 school years. Course work included requirement for a classical education as well as moral instruction and classes in music, drawing, painting and embroidery.*

> *The college operated without interruption through the Civil War. The 1867 epidemic of yellow fever claimed the lives of the college president, several members of the faculty and a number of students. The fall term was delayed until the first frost, which killed the mosquitoes carrying the disease.*

> *'Andrew Female College suffered from competition as other institutions such as the Sam Houston Normal Institute opened*

their doors to women. Enrollment declined after 1872; the school
was closed in 1880. The college property was conveyed to the city
of Huntsville and reopened later that year as the community's
first public school. The structure was eventually relocated and
became a public school for African-American children (1999)

Pleasant Gray, Founder of Huntsville

Besides educational institutions, also of note in Huntsville is a park
near the site of the Pleasant Gray Trading Post dating to the eighteen
thirties. Nearby are statues of Bidai Indians who once traded at the
post. Pleasant Gray named the community Huntsville for his former
home in Alabama. From Alabama, along with his wife, Hannah, Gray
brought his brother, Ephraim, and a good friend, Captain John Crane.
Soon after their arrival, the Grays built a home and Hannah gave birth
to a child, David, the first known birth of an Anglo-American child in
the environs of Huntsville.

Namesakes of Walker County, Two Walkers

Huntsville is the capital of Walker County, which broke off from
Montgomery County in 1846. Walker County has the distinction
among counties spun off initially from the old Washington
Municipality of being named twice, but for different Walkers. The first
to have the honor was Robert J. Walker of Mississippi who introduced
into the United States Congress the resolution to annex Texas to
the Union. As he later was a Unionist during the Civil War or War
Between the States, in 1863 the state legislature changed the honoree
to Samuel H. Walker.

Samuel Walker had a colorful career as a Texas Ranger, fighting
hostile Indians. Then he played a significant role in 1842 helping
Texans repel the Mexican invasion under General Woll. As the war

spread, he was one of the lucky few who survived the infamous Black Bean Episode: captured in Mexico, those who drew a black bean received a sentence of death by a firing squad, those who drew a white bean were saved. Though Samuel Walker managed to outmaneuver death in Mexico in the early eighteen forties, he was not so fortunate a few years later. After performing heroically for General Zachary Taylor's forces in the US Mexican War, Samuel Hamilton Walker died in battle in Mexico. *(See March to Destiny,108)*

A Penitentiary Story

Not only did the US-Mexican War impact the residents of Huntsville and Walker County, but Huntsville also played a vital role later in the Civil War. Especially significant was the role of the State Penitentiary, located in that city. Note the following words from a Huntsville marker expressing the contribution of that institution to the Confederacy:

Penitentiary C.S.A. and Texas Civil War Manufacturing

Inmates, slaves, free men worked in the penitentiary textile factory, main source of clothier goods for Confederate Southwest. Here "king cotton" and wool became millions of yards of cloth and yarn ... uniforms for state troops, Confederate army, needy families of soldiers, cloth sales supported 300 inmates and Union prisoners of war briefly kept there. As Union blockade tightened, army requests flooded in and family cloth distribution rationed. Later financial difficulties and worn machinery caused production lag. A memorial to the Texans who served the Confederacy; erected by the State of Texas 1963. TEXAS CIVIL WAR MANUFACTURING, 1861-65 Heavy military demands-90,000 Texas troops, a 2000 mile coastline-frontier to guard-plus reduced imports, caused a first expansion of Texas industry. Arms and munitions plants were built, and land grants were used to encourage production. Private industry met the need and produced vital supplies for military and civilians. The Confederate quartermaster formed depots and shops for military goods. Production of salt and "king cotton" was hiked to trade for scarce items. Ladies and societies spun and sewed to outfit soldiers.

Huntsville State Park

No visit to Huntsville would be complete without a visit to Huntsville State Park, a 2083-acre recreational area six miles southwest of town. The park was purchased from private owners in 1937 and opened in 1938. The vision for the park came from the Huntsville-Walker County Chamber of Commerce and the Civilian Conservation Corps, CCC, began construction. The park includes a scenic lake, paddle boating, swimming, hiking and horseback riding along beautiful nature trails and ample places for just nature studying. Also pavilions might be rented for various gatherings.

Hezekiah Farris Cabin

No visit to Huntsville would be complete without visiting an authentic relic from the past off the Courthouse Square. This is the original cabin of Hezekiah Farris. Dating to the 1830s, it was the property of one of the pioneers of Farris Community southwest of Huntsville off FM 1791.

Leaving Huntsville and continuing north on I-45 for some thirty miles brings one to Madisonville, completing the circle of the Cradle of Texas Road.

I-45 Corridor and Kimm Thomas

The Cradle of Texas Road is companion to the I-45 Corridor Group consisting of communities along I- 45 stretching from Ennis to Conroe. Kimm Thomas, of the Convention and Visitors Bureau of Huntsville, is exploring possibilities of integrating the interests along both of these roadways.

Selected Sources

Crews, D'Anne McAdams. *Huntsville and Walker County, Texas, a Bicentennial History.* Sam Houston State University Press, 1976.

Montgomery, Robin. *March to Destiny: Cultural Legacy of Stephen F. Austin's Original Colony.* Navasota: R.O.C. Press, 2010.

CONCLUSION

Review and Assessment

There are two ways of reviewing this story. One of these is a traditional review summarizing the story in the order it has been presented, beginning with Madisonville and working our way down highway 90 to 105 and eventually up I-45 to the place of origin. A more innovative and instructive approach employs an historic timeline portraying the sites along the Cradle of Texas Road in the order of their relation to the development of Texas history. Addressed from the latter perspective, it may be shown that togetherness or integration is incorporated through reflection along this road of every significant historical period in Texas. We will portray both approaches, beginning with the framework of the first mentioned. Afterwards will be an assessment of the prospects and possibilities flowing from the emergence of the concept of the Cradle of Texas Road.

— Review in the order presented in the text:—

As we have seen, the first stop of the Cradle of Texas Road from the north is Madisonville, identified with the initial declaration of the Green Flag Republic. This set the stage for our theme of building togetherness through cultural integration. From that start we ventured down highway ninety to Bedias, the namesake of the original inhabitants of the historic era. Then it was on to Roans Prairie and the home of Joshua Hadley, the Alcalde of Washington Municipality, itself the cradle out of which emerged the towns featured in our Cradle Road. Two exotic side trips from there were to Shiro and a story from the Alamo and to Red Top with a look at the formation of Company H of Hood's Brigade. Then it was to Anderson and its identity with the beginning of Texas as a state of the Union, along with a side trip to the site of the old Piedmont Springs Resort. From there we merged into highway 105 at Navasota, the city identified heavily with La Salle and the Bahia Trail. Leaving Navasota the road led to the west and Washington on the Brazos, the Cradle of the Second Republic of Texas.

Retracing our steps to Navasota and continuing east on 105 we passed the historic area of Old Grimes and Montgomery Prairies, home of pioneers of Mexican era Texas, en route to Dobbin followed by Montgomery, where we celebrated the birth of the Lone Star Flag of the Second Republic. Thence it was to Conroe with its plethora of cultural visionaries and on to Cut and Shoot where memories of the mighty Roy Harris yet reign, the man who brought worldwide fame to Cut and Shoot. Finally off 105 we came to Deerwood, a highly influential community of pioneer Hispanics.

From Deerwood we retraced our steps to Conroe and thence up I-45, first to Willis and its claim to fame in terms of basking for a time in the glow of a world class cigar industry. And then there was a bit on old Danville, before venturing through Waverly and New Waverly to finally reach Huntsville, the home of the great Sam Houston. Then it was on north to Madisonville, the place of beginning.

—Review as an Historic Timeline:—

The original Native Americans

In the beginning, there were the Bidai (Bee Dye) Native Americans represented by the community of **Bedias.** These were the original rulers of the land.

The Spanish Era

Then there was representation from Spain, the first European masters of the realm. Representing the Spanish Nation, into the area of our Cradle Road came Luis Moscoso in 1540. With the remains of the Expedition of Hernando de Soto, folklore has it, Moscoso planted in the minds of the Native Americans the legend of the rebirth of de Soto leading to the naming of the **Navasota River**—*Nativity de Soto,* the rebirth of de Soto.

The French Interlude

It was near **Navasota**, the namesake of the Navasota River, where René Robert Cavelier Sieur de La Salle met his demise in 1687, but only after he had placed the mark of the French upon the land that would become Texas. It was La Salle who generated conditions sparking the birth of Spanish *Tejas.*

The First Republic

France and Spain, in turn, gave way to the rise of Mexico under the impact of Miguel Hidalgo. It was a Lt. Colonel of Hidalgo, *Bernardo*

Gutiérrez de Lara, who orchestrated the birth of the First Republic of Texas in 1813. A hybrid state, independent yet attaching its vision to the emerging Mexican Nation, this first state of post-Spanish Texas initially declared its independence at the apex of the Cradle of Texas Road, near **Madisonville.**

Washington Municipality

As Mexico consolidated its claims to Texas, municipalities formed. One of these received the name of Austin Municipality overlapping the area of the Cradle Road. More closely framed to our road was Washington Municipality, carved out of Austin Municipality in 1835. Headquartered at Washington-on-the-Brazos, Washington Municipality's leader was Joshua Hadley whose homestead was near present **Roans Prairie.**

The Second Texas Republic

At **Washington-on-the-Brazos** in 1836, the Second Republic of Texas saw birth. Its military liberator and inaugural president, Sam Houston, is indelibly identified with **Huntsville,** along the Cradle of Texas Road. Also engaging is the story of William B. Travis drawing the line in the sand at the Alamo. Our trip to **Shiro** featured the site where Moses Rose revealed that awesome scene. As the 2nd republic took root, Charles Stewart of **Montgomery** designed the Lone Star Flag. Playing key roles in this era in both Austin and Robertson's Colonies were J.G.W. Pierson and his in-laws of **Montgomery Prairie.**

Texas as a state of the United States

Moving chronologically through history, we next engage the community of **Anderson,** associated via Kenneth Anderson with the rise of Texas as a state of the Union. It was during this era that the venerable Jesse Grimes of **Grimes Prairie** rose to the position of senate pro tempore.

The Confederacy

As Texas became a member of the Confederacy, we see at **Red Top** near Shiro, the site where a tri-county unit was formed, Company H of the famous Hood's Brigade. Outside of Anderson is the location of the famous **Piedmont Springs**, once tantamount to the headquarters of General Magruder's extensive Confederate Command.

Late Nineteenth Century

In the 1890s, a branch of the Cradle Road made world history as the community of **Willis** won multiple prizes for its famous tobacco industry.

20th Century

Endemically associated with Texas history is that of the oil industry. **Conroe** and **Cut and Shoot** share a piece of that exotic history. On the one hand is the winsome story of George W. Strake and his mighty Conroe Oil Field of the 1930s. On the other hand, that oil field reached to Cut and Shoot, generating legends of Texas Folklore in the Big Thicket as a reaction to the sprawling derricks dotting the forests and making life uneasy for the pioneers already ensconced amongst the ocean of trees. Prominent among these legends is that of Roy Harris, Backwoods Battler from Cut and Shoot who in 1958 rose to a shot at the world heavyweight boxing title, later becoming a renaissance man of renown. (One of the authors, Robin Montgomery, just prior to this book, published with Roy Harris, a book entitled *Roy Harris of Cut and Shoot: Texas Backwoods Battler*)

Into the 21st Century

Finally, there is **Deerwood**, a community of the future in the form of the emerging Hispanic majority. In Deerwood, as in nearby Conroe, the vision is of the future, setting the stage for a new birth of freedom through overcoming the straightjacket of polarization.

However its route may be framed, the Cradle of Texas Road is an historic venture laying the groundwork for a noble experiment in cultural integration.

Assessment

Will the hypothesis behind the Cradle of Texas Road prove prophetic? Can a regional constellation of towns and historic sites centered on the social glue of a common historic theme meld into a unit, where each will promote all? As the book goes to press prospects look good. Interviews with representatives along the route have proven fruitful. The larger question, then, seems answered, that there is a basis here for building a sense of regional togetherness, which might serve as a model for cultural integration on a national scale. Remaining is the task to operationalize routine through such projects as making a video and holding regional meetings and events, all of which are in planning as these words are written.

COMPREHENSIVE BIBLIOGRAPHY

Allen, Irene Taylor. *Saga of Anderson: The Proud Story of a Historic Texas Community*. Greenwich Book Publishers, 1958.

Austin, Moses, Stephen Fuller Austin, and Eugene Campbell Barker. *The Austin Papers*. University of Texas, 1926.

Barker, Eugene Campbell. *Mexico and Texas, 1821-1835: University of Texas Research Lectures on the Causes of the Texas Revolution*. Russell & Russell, 1965.

Blair, A. L. *Early History of Grimes County*. Austin, 1930.

Bolton, Herbert. *Texas in the Middle Eighteenth Century: Studies in Spanish Colonial History and Administration*. New York: Russell & Russell, 1962.

Bowman, Bob. "The Lady in Blue." *Texas Escapes Online Magazine*, n.d.

Bugbee, Lester G. "The Old Three Hundred: A List of Settlers in Austin's First Colony." *The Quarterly of the Texas State Historical Association* 1, no. 2 (October 1, 1897): 108–117. doi:10.2307/30242636.

Burleson, Rufus Columbus, and Harry Haynes. *The Life and Writings of Rufus C. Burleson: Containing a Biography of Dr. Burleson by Harry Haynes; Funeral Occasion, with Sermons, Etc; Selected "Chapel Talks;" Dr. Burleson as a Preacher, with Selected Sermons,* 1901.

Carter, Hodding. *Doomed Road of Empire: The Spanish Trail of Conquest.* McGraw-Hill, 1963.

Christian, Carole. "Washington-on-the-Brazos, TX." In *Handbook of Texas,* 6:832–834. Austin: Texas State Historical Association, 1996.

Commission, Grimes County Heritage. *History of Grimes County Texas: Heritage and Progress.* The Commission, 1982.

Crews, D'Anne McAdams. *Huntsville and Walker County, Texas, a Bicentennial History.* Sam Houston State University Press, 1976.

Crittenden, George. "Crittenden Papers." Stoneham, Texas, 1960. Texas Center for Regional Studies Archives.

Eddins, Roy, and Old Settlers and Veterans Association of Falls County Texas. *History of Falls County, Texas,* 1947.

Epperson, Jean. *Lost Spanish Towns: Atacosito and Trinidad De Salcedo.* 2nd ed. Houston: Kemp & Company, 2009.

Foerster, Larry. "Private Collections and Correspondence," 2012.

———. "Short Biography of Richard Williams." In *Cradle of Texas Road,* Supplement Four. iUniverse, 2013.

Foster, William C., and Nicolas de La Salle. *The La Salle Expedition on the Mississippi River: a Lost Manuscript of Nicolas De La Salle, 1682.* Texas State Historical Association, 2003.

Gandy, William Harley. *A History of Montgomery County, Texas*, 1952.

Grimes, Ben. "Ben Grimes Private Papers," n.d. Texas Center for Regional Studies Archives.

Hailey, James. "New Waverly, TX." 4:1006. Austin: Texas State Historical Association, 1996.

Harris, Roy. "On Jack Johnson," n.d.

Harris, Roy, and Robin Montgomery Dr. *Roy Harris of Cut and Shoot: Texas Backwoods Battler.* iUniverse, 2012.

Jackson, Charles Christopher. "Grimes County." In *Handbook of Texas*, 3:342–347. Austin: Texas State Historical Association, 1996.

Jackson, Jack, Manuel de Mier y Terán, Scooter Cheatham, and Lynn Marshall. *Texas by Terán: The Diary Kept by General Manuel De Mier Y Terán on His 1828 Inspection of Texas.* University of Texas Press, 2000.

Jenkins, John. "Hamer, Francis Augustus." In *Handbook of Texas*, 3:426–427. Austin: Texas State Historical Association, 1996.

———. *The Papers of the Texas Revolution, 1835-1836.* Vol. 9. 10 vols. Presidial Press, 1973.

Jordan, Maria. "Maria Jordan, Director, Latino Leadership Roundtable," 2012. http://www.texaslatinoleadership.com.

———. "Texas Latino Leadership Roundtable," n.d. http://www.texaslatinoleadership.com.

Joutel, Henri, and William C. Foster. *The La Salle Expedition to Texas: The Journal of Henri Joutel, 1684-1687.* Texas State Historical Association, 1998.

Kemp, L. W. "Grimes, Jesse." In *Handbook of Texas*, 3:342. Austin: Texas State Historical Association, 1996.

Kemp, Louis Wiltz. *The Signers of the Texas Declaration of Independence*. The Anson Jones press, 1944.

De Leon, Arnoldo. "Mexican Texas." In *The New Handbook of Texas*, 4:689–695. Austin: Texas State Historical Association, 1996.

Lipscomb, Mance Alyn. "A Guide to the Lipscomb-Alyn Collection, 1960-1995." Accessed January 5, 2013. http://www.lib.utexas.edu/taro/utcah/01237/cah-01237.html.

Madison County Historical Commission. *A History of Madison County, Texas*. Dallas: Taylor, 1984.

Montgomery, Andrew. Petition to Legislature 2/3 League of Labor Land Grimes County, Gwyn Morrison Notary Public Grimes County (1855).

Montgomery, Robin. "Conroe Courier," n.d.

———. *Cut 'n Shoot, Texas: The Roy Harris Story*. Eakin Press, 1984.

———. *Historic Montgomery County: An Illustrated History of Montgomery County, Texas*. Historical Pub. Network, 2003.

———. *Indians & Pioneers in Original Montgomery County: By Robin Montgomery*. Historical Pub. Network, 2006.

———. *March to Destiny: Cultural Legacy of Stephen F. Austin's Original Colony*. Navasota: R.O.C. Press, 2010.

———. "Newspaper Coloumns from Conroe Courier and on Texas Center for Regional Studies Website," n.d.

———. "Securing the Original Boarders of Montgomery County." In

Historic Montgomery County: An Illustrated History of Montgomery County, Texas, 43–46. Historical Pub. Network, 2003.

———. *The History of Montgomery County*. Jenkins Pub. Co., 1975.

———. *Tortured Destiny: Lament of a Shaman Princess*. Christian Ages Press, 2001.

Montgomery, Robin, Joy Montgomery, and Texas Center for Regional Studies. *Navasota*. Arcadia Publishing, 2012.

Morrell, Z. N. *FLOWERS AND FRUITS FROM THE WILDERNESS*. Boston: Gould and Lincoln, 1872.

Parker, James W., and Rachel Parker Plummer. *The Rachel Plummer Narrative: A Stirring Narrative of Adventure, Hardship and Privation in the Early Days of Texas, Depicting Struggles with the Indians and Other Adventures ...*, 1926.

Perrigo, Lynn Irwin. *Our Spanish Southwest*. Banks Upshaw, 1960.

Pierson, Edwin G. "Pierson, John Goodloe Warren." In *Handbook of Texas*, 5:197–198. Austin: Texas State Historical Association, 1996.

Powell, Guy E. *Latest Aztec Discoveries: Origin and Untold Riches*. Naylor Company, 1970.

Ray, Worth Stickley. *Austin Colony Pioneers: Including History of Bastrop, Fayette, Grimes, Montgomery, and Washington Counties, Texas*. W. S. Ray, 1949.

De Shields, James T. *Border Wars of Texas: Being an Authentic and Popular Account, in Chronological Order, of the Long and Bitter Conflict Waged Between Savage Indian Tribes and the Pioneer Settlers of Texas*. The Herald company, 1912.

Standifer, Mary. "Dodson, Sarah Randoph Bradley." In *Handbook of Texas*, 2:668. Austin: Texas State Historical Association, 1996.

State, Texas (Republic). Dept. of. "Texas (Republic). Department of State: An Inventory of Department of State, Republic of Texas Election Returns at the Texas State Archives, 1835-1845." Accessed January 5, 2013. http://www.lib.utexas.edu/taro/tslac/30102/tsl-30102.html.

Steen, Ralph. "Convention of 1836." In *Handbook of Texas*, 3:297. Austin: Texas State Historical Association, 1996.

Texas, and D. E. Simmons. *Index to Gammel's Laws of Texas, 1822-1905…* H.P.N. Gammel, 1906.

Various. "Pan American Roundtable, Conroe," n.d.

———. "Websites: Marlen Tajeda, Marisa Olvares Rummell, Chikawa, and Rita Wiltz," n.d.

Weber, David J. *The Mexican Frontier, 1821-1846: The American Southwest Under Mexico*. UNM Press, 1982.

Weddle, Robert S. "Moscoso Alvarado, Luis De (1505-1551)." In *Handbook of Texas*, 4:851. Austin: Texas State Historical Association, 1996.

Wilbarger, John Wesley. *Indian Depredations in Texas: Reliable Accounts of Battles, Wars, Adventures, Forays, Murders, Massacres, Etc., Etc., Together with Biographical Sketches of Many of the Most Noted Indian Fighters and Frontiersmen of Texas*. The Steck Co., 1889.

Winkler, E. W. "Documents Relating to the Organization of the Muicipality of Washington, Texas." *Southwestern Historical Quarterly* 10, no. 1 (July 1906): 96–100.

Zuber, William Physick. "A Guide to the Zuber (William Physick) Papers, Ca. 1820-1923." Accessed January 5, 2013. http://www.lib.utexas.edu/taro/utcah/03199/cah-03199.html.

"Hood's Texas Brigade." 3:687. Austin: Texas State Historical Association, 1996.

PART II.
Cradle of Texas Road:
Supplements

CRADLE OF TEXAS ROAD, SUPPLEMENT ONE

La Salle's Texas Legacy

by Robin Montgomery

T he legacy of René Robert Cavelier Sieur de La Salle is of phenomenal proportions. It shaped the foreign policies of multiple nations spanning nearly 200 years. These policies, whether of France, Spain, Mexico, the First and Second Republics of Texas, the State of Texas or the United States, developed the story of Texas along a path that La Salle blazed. We will look at each of these stories in turn, against the theme of the Cradle of Texas.

La Salle, Progenitor of Louisiana

In 1682, traveling from the Illinois Country, La Salle led an expedition to the mouth of the Mississippi River. This was the first land expedition to discover the broader dimensions of the river, although in 1519 a Spanish Naval Expedition under Alonso Alvarez de Pineda had discovered and named it the Rio del Espíritu Santo. Putting Spain and the rest of the world on notice, La Salle staked a claim for France of all the lands drained by the mighty river. Then, for his sovereign, Louis XIV and his wife Anne, he named that vast area Louisiana.

Rise of the Original Texas

Returning to France, La Salle gathered an expedition then set out to revisit the Mississippi. Missing his mark, on 20 February 1685 he landed instead far to the west at Matagorda Bay. Not only did he miscalculate his destination, but various mishaps resulted in only one of his four ships remaining until the final landing. That one, the Belle, soon was wrecked, leaving the remainder of his expedition stranded. Hence off Garcitas Creek, which flows into Lavaca Bay, La Salle established a base of operations, which he christened Fort Saint Louis.

Great was the alarm of the Spanish, from their headquarters in Mexico City, on learning of this French incursion into territory that they claimed as part of New Spain (now called Mexico). La Salle's mishap alerted Spain to the importance of the area above the Rio Grande, which river marked the northern limit of their official presence at that time. While the Spanish searched for him by land and sea, La Salle led several expeditions inland. Most importantly for this study, the first was westward to the Rio Grande.1 Then he traveled eastward nearly to his goal of the Mississippi. On a final expedition on 19 March 1687, near present Navasota, a quarrel among his followers resulted in the death of the great explorer.2

But La Salle's death was just the beginning of the far-reaching repercussions of his expedition. On finding the remains of Fort St. Louis in 1689, Frenchmen from La Salle's last expedition brought to the Spanish a chieftain from the Hasinai branch of the Caddo Nation. It was this chieftain who invited them to establish a mission in his land. This the Spanish did. In 1690, the expedition of Alonso de Leon and Father Damien Massanet established beyond the present city of Crocket the Mission *San Francisco de las Tejas*. Here the Indians referred to the Spanish as *Tayshas*, which means in Spanish, *Tejas*. The English translation is Texas. Directly related to La Salle's last expedition, the Spanish established what came to be the Spanish Province of *Tejas* and, along the way, blazed the La Bahia Trail. Thus inaugurated was the Cradle of Texas.3

Rise of the First Republic of Texas, the Green Flag Republic

In the 1720s, the first capital of the Province of Texas was established at Los Adaes in the western portion of present Louisiana.4 In 1762, France ceded Louisiana to Spain, thus reducing Spanish fears of French encroachment on their territory. Consequently, in 1773, the capital of Texas was moved west to San Antonio, a city founded in 1718. Here a hardy and independent breed of Spanish, forged on the frontier, emerged. These were the *Tejanos*.5

Meanwhile, the United States was also harvesting a generation of hardy souls, searching for adventure and a cause. They found a cause when France, upon once more becoming the proprietors of Louisiana in 1800, three years later sold the vast region to the United States. Here we return to the La Salle factor.

La Salle, it will be recalled, explored to the Rio Grande, thus establishing the French claim to that extent. It was for this reason that upon orchestrating the Louisiana Purchase from the emperor, Napoleon I of France, US President Thomas Jefferson considered that river as the boundary with Spanish Texas. However, given the diplomatic stalemate, it was decided to finesse the issue of the border in order to consummate the agreement.6 But the issue would not go away, leaving it up to military officials on the scene in 1806 to fashion a neutral ground, far from the Rio Grande, between the Sabine

River and the Arroyo Hondo, the latter stream near the Red River. While cooperation extended to joint US-Spanish patrols on occasion extricating undesirable elements from the zone, by 1812 cooperation had broken down, thus resuscitating the LaSalle-based Rio Grande argument.

It was within this volatile political atmosphere that a priest in Mexico, Miguel Hidalgo, on 16 September 1810 garnered a rag tag army, sparking the 11-year struggle to win Mexican independence from Spain. Before his betrayal and execution, Hidalgo commissioned Bernardo Gutiérrez de Lara a Lt. Colonel and sent him to the US seeking support. There, adventurers were in abundance ready to claim the mandate La Salle had forged. Therefore, with an army of restless United States citizens, Indians and *Tejanos*, Gutiérrez conquered San Antonio on 1 April, 1813 to establish the First Republic of Texas. From the start, this Green Flag Republic was plagued with dissension leading to the republic's demise at the Battle of Medina on 18 August 1813. Later, in 1821, though, the eventual liberator of Mexico, Agustin de Iturbide, gave official sanction to Gutiérrez's efforts in support of Mexican Independence.7

Rise of the Second Republic of Texas, the Lone Star Republic

Even as an independent Mexico consolidated its power, the issue of its border with Texas waxed volatile. This remained so even though one of the last acts of Spain was to consummate the Adams-Onis Treaty. This marked, in part, the Sabine as the border with the United States, while Spain ceded Florida to the US. Though Spain ratified the treaty in 1821 as a last gasp of its control of Texas, Mexico, Spain's successor, hesitated until 1831 to follow suit.

Meanwhile, public opinion in the US was not uniformly favorable to surrendering Texas. For instance, the treaty sparked the Dr. James

Long Expedition to try, unsuccessfully, to free Texas from Spain. Even after Mexico began allowing empressarios such as Stephen F. Austin to colonize Texas, just below the surface of US public opinion festered the desire to free Texas. In 1826, the issue caught fire with the rise in Texas of the Fredonian Republic. A disgruntled empressario, Haden Edwards, and his brother, Benjamin, along with a goodly collection of followers, sought to garner an empire stretching from the Sabine to the Rio Grande.

Though the Fredonians quickly failed, the revolt placed the Mexican government on alert. Adding to Mexican insecurities were US newspaper reports that the new president, Andrew Jackson, intended to resurrect the La Salle factor as his rationale to take Texas with the Rio Grande as the southern border. Both the Jackson and John Quincy Adams administrations did indeed make explicit offers to buy Texas. Adding fuel to the fire along the way was the Mexican ruling of 6 April, 1830 greatly limiting further efforts at emigration from the US.

This was the atmosphere that led in 1836 to the Mexican siege of the Alamo and the following pivotal Battle of San Jacinto, which generated an Independent Texas. After that battle, what has been called the "Treaties" of Velasco, one public, the other private, listed the victor's terms of surrender. Among those were the demands that Mexican troops retire south of the Rio Grande and that the Rio Grande would be the southern border. At the First Congress of the Republic of Texas, the members also made explicit their insistence on the Rio Grande as the border.8

The border issue continued to fester, even as Texas accepted the invitation of the United States to become a state in the union. Texas claimed the Rio Grande, while Mexico insisted on the Nueces River to the north. Furthermore, Mexico had never recognized the Texas Republic as an independent nation. Thus did echoes from La Salle yet resound over Texas and Mexico. Soon those echoes would crescendo into the sounds of a major war.

Annexation of Texas and the US-Mexican War

Although President John Tyler orchestrated the annexation of Texas in late 1845 it was President James K. Polk who stroked the fires of war. General Zachary Taylor was his means. Polk sent Taylor with a military force straight to the heart of the wound throbbing in the collective soul of Mexico, the disputed territory between the Nueces and the Rio Grande. There, Mexicans fired upon US forces. This President Polk used as his pretext for war.

And what a war that of 1846-48 was! The US gained all or part of the states of New Mexico, Arizona, California, Nevada, Utah, Colorado and Wyoming while making the annexation of Texas complete. And finally, the La Salle factor bore further fruit for the United States as Mexico at last succumbed to the Rio Grande as the border with Texas.9

La Salle, the Confederacy and Cinco de Mayo

Not only did the La Salle factor play into the foreign policies of numerous political entities over the one hundred and sixty six years from 1682-1848. Echoes from the La Salle effect also set the stage for an annual and major holiday, growing in popularity. Celebrating the togetherness generated through a marriage of French Revolutionary Tradition with that of Mexico is this holiday, known as Cinco de Mayo.

The initial setting for this cultural convergence was Puebla, Mexico, on 5 May 1862. On that day, French troops of Napoleon III of

France met those of Mexico's Texas-born General, Ignacio Zaragosa. Though outnumbered immensely, Zaragosa prevailed. And great was the fallout worldwide. This was the first loss for mighty French Army in nearly fifty years. Though France eventually reached its goal of occupying Mexico City, results of the victory were transient, for the Battle of Puebla on Cinco de Mayo had diminished France's ability to support the Confederacy. This bought time for Abraham Lincoln to conclude the Civil War and muster troops to monitor the Mexican border. Thus did the Battle of Puebla end for Napoleon III his dream of resurrecting the vision of his uncle, Napoleon I. That vision had entailed French dominance in the areas which La Salle had claimed for France so long ago.*10*

But Cinco de Mayo has come to transcend these points of conflict. Instead, it blends the vision of freedom inspired by the Battle of Puebla and the French, American and Texas Revolutions into a beckon of light celebrating cultural togetherness.

What mighty events were set in motion, for Texas and the world, when a valiant explorer lost his way, to end his life's journey near Navasota: La Salle's death fostered a proverbial cradle nurturing a road to freedom.

Endnotes

1   See map, page 113 in William C. Foster, (ed.), Johanna S. Warren, (trans.), *The La Salle Expedition to Texas: The Journal of Henri Joutel 1684-1687*(Austin: Texas State Historical Association, 1998)—Whether La Salle, himself, reached the Rio Grande is unclear to some, but it is agreed that at least "La Salle's soldiers" did so. (See pp37-38)

2   Herbert Bolton, "The Location of LaSalle's Colony on the Gulf of Mexico," pp171-189 in *The Southwestern Historical Quarterly*,27 (Jan., 1924), no.3.(W. C. Foster,op.cit.,concurs,33-34) http://texashistory. unt.edu/ark:/67531/metapth101086/m1/177/med_res/ viewed 1/18/12. For a summary of the contrary positions, see Robin Montgomery, *March to Destiny: Cultural Legacy of Stephen F. Austin's Original Colony*(Navasota: ROC Press, 2010), 56-62

3   An intriguing discussion of this sequence of events is in Hodding Carter, *Doomed Road of Empire: The Spanish Trail of Conquest*(New York: McGraw-Hill, 1963), 45-47.

4   A scintillating read of this era is Robert Carlton Clark, "Louis Juchereau de Saint-Denis and the Re-Establishment of the Texas Missions," pp2-26 in The *Quarterly of the Texas State Historical Association*, 6(July 1902), no.1.—The author was the first to note that the expedition "determined the ownership of Texas", shaping the course of North American history.

5   For perspective on the rise of the Tejanos, see "Tejano Roots, 1700-1848", chapter four of Robin Montgomery, *March to Destiny*.

6   The classic essay on the politics of the border issues inherent in Jefferson's Louisiana Purchase is Isaac Joslin Cox, "The Louisiana-Texas Frontier, II", pp. 1-42 in *The Southwestern Historical Quarterly*,17(July 1913), no.1

7 For the cultural context surrounding the First Republic, see Robin Montgomery, *Celebrating Togetherness: Anglos, Mexicans and the 1st Republic of Texas, 1813* (Richards, TX: Texas Center for Regional Studies, 2011)

8 See, for instance, Jesús F. de la Teja, "Texas in the Age of Mexican Independence," Handbook of Texas Online (http://www.tshaonline. org/handbook/online/articles/uptsd), accessed 1/19/12 published by Texas State Historical Society.

9 For a succinct, yet instructive, treatment of the US-Mexican War, see Richard Griswold del Castillo, "Treaty of Guadalupe Hidalgo", on the PBS website. http://www.pbs.org/kera/usmexicanwar/war/wars_end_guadalupe.html accessed 1/17/12

10 See Ignacio Gonzalez, "The Significance of Cinco de Mayo." www. Aztec.net, http://www.mexica.net/literat/cinco.php accessed 1/18/12

CRADLE OF TEXAS ROAD, SUPPLEMENT TWO

Celebrating Togetherness: Mexicans, Anglos & the First Republic of Texas

By Robin Montgomery

Author's note: The first stop of the Cradle Road is linked to this event. In October 1812, at Trinidad, outside of Madisonville, "The Republican Army of the North" first declared the Independence of Texas, at that time from the Trinity River to the Sabine.

Preface

Entering the second decade of the twenty-first century, the United States is being polarized alarmingly along racial and cultural lines. Of immediate concern is the widening breach between Hispanics and those of Anglo-American heritage. University of New Mexico professor, Charles Truxillo, for instance, is projecting that before the end of the 21st century a new country, to be called "The Republic of the North", will be carved out of the southwestern states of the US and the northern states of Mexico.

This study addresses the crisis of social fragmentation in our country by laying an historical foundation upon which to resurrect a sense of common national identity. Explored here are the shared roots of Anglo-American and Hispanic-American cultures in events surrounding the rise of the First Republic of Texas. Emphasized is the direct link between these events and the drive for Mexican independence from Spain, which Father Miguel Hidalgo initiated on 16 September 16th, 1810.

By portraying the decisive role of the blending of Anglo and Hispanic cultures in the rise of the first republic, the study is "Celebrating Togetherness".

Introduction

In 1813, Texas was a part of Mexico, which was in turn a colony of Spain. On April 6th of that year, the first independent Republic of Texas was established. Earlier, seeking to arouse his Mexican countrymen to the cause of independence, the soon to be president of the republic expressed the multicultural mix of his followers:

> *"Rise en masse, soldiers and citizens: unite in the holy cause of our country! I am now marching to your succor with a respectable force of American volunteers who left their homes and families to take up our cause, to fight for our liberty. They are the free descendants of the men who fought for the independence of the United States: and as brothers and inhabitants of the same continent they have drawn their swords with a hearty good will in the defense of the cause of humanity: and in order to drive the tyrannous Europeans beyond the Atlantic." (bib.: "The First Republic of Texas")*

The man expressing these words was Bernardo Gutiérrez de Lara, whose mentor and inspiration was Miguel Hidalgo, a lowly parish priest in Dolores Mexico. In that town, on September 16, 1810, Hidalgo had given vent to words known to all lovers of freedom as the "Grito de Dolores", a cry for freedom under the banner of the Patroness of the Americas, "Our Lady of Guadalupe". "Long live Religion, long live America," he cried. Hidalgo's message spread across the length and breadth of his country, giving birth to a movement that by 1821 resulted, finally, in freedom for Mexico from its Spanish overlords. In the early stages of that struggle, Hidalgo commissioned Bernardo Gutiérrez as a Lt. Colonel in his Army.

Exploring the link between Hidalgo, Gutiérrez, and volunteers from the United States in establishing the first Texas Republic is the primary thrust of our story. We will begin with an initial survey of the historical class structure of Mexico then proceed to the events giving rise to the "Grito de Dolores". We will follow with a survey of the repercussions of Hidalgo's Grito including the rise of Gutiérrez and the establishment of the first Republic of Texas. The conclusion will explore the significance of these events for the blending of Hispanic and Anglo-American cultures.

Mexico (New Spain): From Cortéz to Hidalgo: Founding of New Spain & its Culture

In 1519, an adventurer based in Spanish-controlled Cuba, Hernán Cortéz, undertook the leadership of an expedition to the coast of the mainland to the west. Upon landing, he established a town he called Vera Cruz, the True Cross. Named for its colonial master, Spain, the surrounding land was known as New Spain. By 1522, Cortéz and his army had conquered the dominant civilization of the vast area of New Spain, the Aztec Empire.

Over the next three centuries, a highly stratified society emerged in the ever-expanding Spanish Colony. At the apex of society were those who enjoyed the accident of having been born on the peninsular of Spain. They were known as *peninsulares*, and they held the key political positions of the land, starting with the position of viceroy, vice king, the direct representative of the king of Spain. Next in the social hierarchy were those of essentially pure Spanish descent but born in New Spain. There were called *criollos* (creoles). Finally came the mixed bloods, those of some Spanish descent. First among these were the *mestizos*, of Spanish and Indian blood, and then there were the *mulattoes*, a mixture of Spanish and African-American lineage. Holding the bottom rung of society were the Indians and African-Americans.

Over time the position of the Indian in New Spain became progressively more untenable. Not only did diseases brought by the Europeans, for which the Indians had no immunity, decimate their numbers but also the Indians fell liable for tribute in time and labor to their Spanish masters.

Sustenance to cope with this condition of servitude came for the Indian in a dramatic fashion one day in January 1531. An Indian peasant, Juan Diego, now St. Juan Diego, was worshipping at the shrine of the Indian serpent goddess. To his grand surprise, amid bright light and bird song, the Virgin Mary appeared to him. She requested that Juan tell the Spanish authorities of her, asking them build a shrine to her on the sacred hill on which she stood. The faithful Indian did his best to meet the grand lady's request, but alas, was unable to meet success.

Undaunted, the lady appeared to him a second time in the same place. This time she asked him to climb to the top of the hill and there pick red roses, placing them in his cloak. Although it was the dead of winter and besides, only cactus had ever grown on this hilltop, the faithful Indian obeyed. And the roses were there. Placing them in his cloak as requested, he presented them to the priest. To the surprise of all, appearing on the cloak were not roses by an image of the lady made without human hands.

Placed in the nearby town of Guadalupe, the cloak became a shrine known as the "Virgin of Guadalupe." Copies of the shrine appeared throughout the Americas. Worship of the Patroness of the Americas had begun.

Change Agents

The beginning of the end of the highly stratified society of New Spain came in 1808. In that year, the French Emperor, Napoleon Bonaparte, placed his brother, Joseph, on the throne of Spain. Napoleon took the legitimate heir apparent to the Spanish crown, Ferdinand VII, into captivity in France.

The reaction in New Spain to Napoleon's coup was along class lines. The *peninsulares* supported the viceroyalty, hoping that way to continue to exercise power. On the other hand, the *criollos* and higher-level *mestizos*, for the most part, looked to find some way to gain independence for New Spain in the name of the deposed king Ferdinand. The lower level *mestizos* and *mulattoes*, Indians and African-Americans, generally remained out of play of the politics, living as they had for centuries.

Rise of Miguel Hidalgo

Miguel Hidalgo was born on May 8, 1753, near Guanajuato, New Spain. The early years of his education were at Valladolid, now called Morelia, and he became a priest in 1779. Along the way, he learned several Indian dialects as well as French.

The latter language he used as the bridge to take him to knowledge of the philosophy behind the French Revolution of 1789. Reading this literature was considered sacrilege in New Spain in those times.

By 1810, Hidalgo had become a priest in the village of Dolores, New Spain, not far from his native Guanajuato. He would on occasion travel to the nearby town of Queretaro where he would visit with other *criollos* and more cultured *mestizos* of like-minded philosophical bent. It was on these occasions that he became involved with a group bent on revolting against the French-supported peninsulare establishment. With a loose coalition including most prominently a criollo military officer named Ignacio Allende, Hidalgo marked December 1810 as the time for the revolt to begin. Alas, however, word of the plan leaked to the peninsulare authorities prompting a momentous decision from Hidalgo, would he run or would he fight?

Hidalgo chose to fight. It was thus on September 16, 1810, that Miguel Hidalgo rang the bell summoning his lower class flock and announced that the time had come for revolution in the name of religion and Independence, as subjects of King Ferdinand VII of Spain. Animated, his flock followed him, bent on taking Mexico City. Along the way, they took on a banner emblazoned with the Image of the Virgin of Guadalupe. In the name of the holy catholic religion, they would rout the Spanish royalists, now under the influence of the French apostles of the secular ideas of the French Revolution and Enlightenment.

As Hidalgo and Allende led their undisciplined army toward Mexico City, violence and massacres were rife everywhere in their path. So much so that on the outskirts of the city, with victory in his grasp, Hidalgo hesitated, to the chagrin of the more military-minded Allende, and decided to forfeit a sure victory. Instead, he turned his army around and headed for Texas, seeking to gain support in the United States.

By early 1811, Hidalgo's Army had lost several key battles but had managed to get to the state of Coahuila just below the line of the present border of Texas. During this time, Coahuila and nearby Nueva Leon as well Nueva Santander north of the Rio Grande were sympathetic to the insurgent cause. So was Texas.

Meanwhile, in San Antonio

In 1773, San Antonio had become the capital of the Province of Texas. As Hidalgo was making his way north, the Spanish Governor in charge of the state was Manuel Salcedo. On January 21, 1811, Juan Bautista de Las Casas initiated a coup de etat against Salcedo. Salcedo received a sentence from the new administration to house arrest in a hacienda or plantation outside of Monclova, Coahuila. Managing the hacienda was an ally of Hidalgo named Ignacio Elizondo.

The sojourn of Salcedo at the hacienda of Elizondo was destined to be short-lived, for on March 2, 1811, the regime of Las Casas suffered defeat. Juan Manuel Zambrano, a loyalist of the royalist cause, took his place. The new regime reversed the sentence of Manuel Salcedo, and then sent troops to the Elizondo hacienda to release the former governor. Their task was easy for Elizondo, the overseer of Salcedo, had deserted the insurgent cause by the time of their arrival.

The fate of Miguel Hidalgo, Spring and Summer 1811

These events coincided with the arrival of the main forces of Miguel Hidalgo and Ignacio Allende into northern New Spain. Hearing that Hidalgo was in the area, the traitor to Hidalgo's cause, Elizondo, mustered a force together, and under the authority of a revitalized Manuel Salcedo, succeeded in luring Hidalgo and his army into a trap and apprehending them. The patriotic captives were escorted to Chihuahua where Salcedo presided over their trial, sentencing Hidalgo, Allende and the main leaders to death. Not only were they killed, but Hidalgo and Allende, along with two other members of Hidalgo's high command, had their heads severed from their bodies and placed on pillars in public at Guanajuato. There they remained for some ten years.

The Era of Mexican and Texas Patriots Together: Enter Bernardo Gutiérrez de Lara

Bernardo Gutiérrez de Lara was a blacksmith of *criollo* lineage who spread revolutionary flyers within areas in the vicinity of the eastern reaches of the Rio Grande. As Hidalgo made his way north, Bernardo greeted him, receiving in return a commission as a Lt. Col. Hidalgo also made Bernardo his envoy to the United States. Although it was just after Hidalgo suffered death, Bernardo Gutiérrez did indeed make his way to the United States where he visited with Secretary of State James Monroe. A representative of Monroe, William Shaler, subsequently joined Gutiérrez in Louisiana and accompanied him to Texas, entering the state in August 1812.

With Bernardo Gutiérrez as co-leader of forces was an officer of the United States Army, Augustus Magee, who soon resigned his United States' commission. The resultant Gutiérrez-Magee Expedition was able easily to capture Nacogdoches, and then it was on to the Trinity where they overcame the Spanish forces of the fortress of Trinidad. From here they headed for San Antonio. En route, as they approached the Colorado River, word came that Manuel Salcedo, now back in power as governor of Texas, was awaiting them. Hence the expedition turned south toward Goliad and captured the Bahia Presidio there.

Governor Manuel Salcedo's Army soon laid siege to the fortress of Bahia. However, with time, the revolutionaries ventured out victorious and set their sights on San Antonio. It was as they neared that city that

Bernardo Gutiérrez spread the word to the citizens of San Antonio, quoted in the introduction that he was on the way with support from freedom-loving Anglo-Americans and Native Americans.

The Green Flag Republic

By early April, the expedition had achieved success. On April 6, 1813, Gutiérrez proclaimed the Republic of Texas and proceeded to write a constitution. Before reaching San Antonio, Gutiérrez's military cohort, Augustus Magee, had died during the Bahia siege. However, the green flag that Magee had fashioned at the beginning of the Gutiérrez-Magee expedition in honor of his Irish ancestry symbolized the new republic, indeed known as the "Green Flag Republic." Thus, the first Republic of Texas was headed by a Mexican, heir of Miguel Hidalgo's revolution, and under a symbol of Irish-American lineage.

As President of Texas, one of the first acts of Gutiérrez was to bring to justice Manuel Salcedo and his cohorts, sentencing them to be imprisoned outside of the capital city. Thus did Bernardo Gutiérrez avenge the death of the executioner of Miguel Hidalgo, Ignacio Allende, and their key followers. Unfortunately, this great deed was mishandled as Antonio Delgado, the man in charge of the forces escorting Manuel Salcedo and company, had revenge on his mind. Salcedo had been responsible for the execution of Delgado's father. Consequently, just outside of San Antonio, Delgado called for Salcedo and his colleagues to dismount and proceeded, with the help of his followers, to slit their throats. Not only this, but the executioners returned to San Antonio to brag about the matter. This gruesome incident led to the alienation of many of the Anglo-Americans who were affiliated with the Gutiérrez government and they consequently left the city and state.

Whether Gutiérrez had sanctioned the massacre of the Salcedo group is yet debated among historians. What seems for sure, however, is that this was one of the reasons that he was forced from office on August 4, 1813.

The Battle of Medina

The man replacing Bernardo Gutiérrez de Lara as President of the Republic of Texas was José Alvarez de Toledo. After an initial skirmish with a force under Ignacio Elizondo, on August 18, 1813, Toledo led some 1400 hundred troops into battle against the royalist General Joaquin Arredondo. This was near the Medina River. In the bloodiest battle in Texas history, all but about 100 of Toledo's followers suffered death.

A primary cause of the debacle lay in Toledo's decision to divide his forces by race. He created separate groups of insurgent Mexicans, Indians and Anglo-Americans. There was at least one African American among Toledo's troops, a man named Thomas. The racial division of forces proved highly inefficient, as representatives of these groups had been used to working together. Apart, they were ineffective. United upon their entry into San Antonio they had successfully proclaimed the first Republic of Texas. Later, however, divided, the republic fell, defeated. This defeat, however, failed to sever the link between Gutiérrez and Texas.

Gutierrez supports later filibustering expeditions into Texas

In 1817 Francisco Mina, a Spaniard, sought to continue the Hidalgo rebellion and engaged royalist forces in southern Texas. Lending liaison aid and support to the unsuccessful Mina Expedition was Gutiérrez.

The First Lone Star Republic

During 1819 to 1821, Dr. James Long embraced filibustering expeditions to Texas. The first expedition set up bases along both the Trinity and Brazos Rivers while the last operated at Bolivar Point off Galveston Bay. Representing the government of Dr. Long was a flag emblazoned with a white lone star against an immediate red background coupled to red and white stripes. Alternately, for a time, was a solid red flag with a white star.

Playing an endemic role with Long was the peripatetic Bernardo Gutiérrez. Gutiérrez was a member of Long's council of advisors and slated to be vice president, should the revolution have succeeded in implementing the second Republic of Texas.

Interestingly, the person whom Long projected to fill the role of president was José Felix Trespalacios of the Mexican state of Chihuahua, a revolutionary also drawn from circles heir to Hidalgo. By the time of the Long Expedition, Trespalacios had been imprisoned several times by royalist forces; the last time he was placed among survivors of the ill-fated Mina Expedition. Managing to escape, Trespalacios made his way to New Orleans. There he made contact with James Long, becoming the nominal commander of the Long Expedition. He survived to become the first president of the post Spanish era Mexican State of Coahuila y Texas.

Gutiérrez de Lara recognized in an independent Mexico

The final liberator of Mexico from Spanish rule was Augustin de Iturbide, who formally recognized the efforts of Gutiérrez de Lara for his significant accomplishments toward Mexican Independence. Reflective of the gratefulness of his country, Gutiérrez received election to the governorship of the Mexican State of Tamaulipas in

1824 as well as being named commandant general of that state in the following year.

In Conclusion

It has been shown that by extension, Hidalgo's revolution was intrinsically intertwined with events in Texas and the United States. Linked to Bernardo Gutiérrez de Lara, the phase of the revolution in Texas reflected an intercultural mix, militarily, socially, politically and in terms of religion, a glorious chapter in the history of both Mexico and the United States.

Truly, on September 16th and on April 6th in unity we can proclaim, "Viva Hidalgo, Viva Mexico, Viva Texas and *Viva los Estados Unidos*"!

Selected Sources

BOOKS:

Carter, Hodding. *Doomed Road of Empire*. New York: McGraw Hill, 1963.

Foote, Henry Stuart, *Texas and The Texans*. Vol. I; Austin: The Steck co., 1935.

Garrett, Julia K., *Green Flag Over Texas*: NY-Dallas: Cordova Press, 1939

Montgomery, Robin. *The History of Montgomery County, TX*. Austin: Jenkins co., 1974, & sesquicentennial ed., Conroe Sesquicentennial Committee, 1986.

Parkes, Henry Bamford. *A History of Mexico*. 3rd edition; Boston: Houghton Mifflin co., 1960.

Putnam, Robert. *Bowling Alone: The Collapse and Revival of American Community*. New York: Simon & Shuster, 2000.

Yoakum, H., *History of Texas*. Austin: Steck co., 1855.

ARTICLES:

Gutierrez de Lara, " 1815, Aug.1 J.B. Gutierrez de Lara to the Mexican Congress. Account of Progress of Revolution from the Beginning." pp. 4-29 in *Lamar Papers*, vol. I,(Austin-NY: Pemberton Press, 1968.)

"The First Republic of Texas". New Spain-Index. Sons of Dewitt Colony. http://www.tamu.edu/faculty/ccbn/dewitt/Spain2.htm

Thornhoff, "Medina, Battle of". Handbook of Texas Online. http://www.tshaonline.org/handbook/online/articles/MM/gfm1.html

Truxillo, Charles. "The Inevitability of a Mexican Nation in the American Southwest & Northern Mexico." My Space. http://us.mg4.yahoo. com/dc/launch?.gx=1&rand=f09i257071

Walker, Henry P., "William McLane's Narrative of the Magee-Gutiérrez Expedition", 1812-1813". Quarterly of The Southwestern Historical Society, Vol.LXVI,no.2(Oct.1962); Vol.LXVI, no.3 (Jan.1963); Vol. LXVI, no.4(April,1963).

Warren, Gaylord, "Long Expedition." Handbook of Texas Online. http:// www.tshaonline.org/handbook/online/articles/LL/gy11.html

CRADLE OF TEXAS ROAD, SUPPLEMENT THREE

The Deerwood Community

by Maria Baños Jordan

D eerwood has over 350 families, probably about 1300 residents. Committed resident volunteers have established a close-knit network of support among each other over the years. Reminiscent of American small towns of the past, neighbors help each other through times of crisis and need, and they gather often to celebrate family and community through community festivals and development projects that lift their modest community. Mr. and Mrs. Sergio Castillo were one of the first families who settled in the community. "Don Sergio" as he is known by everyone in the community, remembers cutting down the first trees to build the small community center. "Doña Yolanda" is present at every gathering, and offers guidance to new young families. Residents have great reverence for these founding members of Deerwood.

Deerwood is known as the hometown of hundreds of Montgomery County Latinos that today trace their beginnings to this still emerging community. One such former resident, Ms. Liz Rubio, was one of the first children born in Deerwood to struggling immigrant parents. She recalls being the only Latina student in her elementary class. Today, she is a mother and student completing her studies at the University of Houston with plans to enter law school. In 2011 she was one of 40 Hispanics in the U.S. to be selected to the prestigious Harvard Hispanic Leadership Program. Like many second generation Americans, she is fulfilling the hopes of her hardworking parents.

The Deerwood Familia Project has included dedicated work from Devery Johnson with the Conroe Montgomery County Library, Alejandra Tapia, Rod Chaves, and Mary Byrne with Conroe ISD, Mark Bosma and Juanita Stanley with Montgomery County, Becky Gustamante with Lone Star College-Montgomery, and volunteers, Lolita Lopez Cardenas, Diana Velardo, JD, Nancy Bocanegra, and Dr. Wally Wilkerson. This effort is helping to encourage other communities struggling to connect across cultures.

Texas Latino Leadership Roundtable

Maria Baños Jordan is Executive Director and Cofounder of Texas Latino Leadership Roundtable, along with fellow cofounders and members, Juanita Estrella Zavala, Phillip Arroyo, Mario Rosales, Tomas Baños, Maribel Garza Scarbrough, and Lupe Martinez. The Texas Latino Leadership Roundtable support role in a changing county will be to provide a perspective on important local issues. In addition to the Leadership Roundtable, Maria Baños Jordan's commitment to Latino family issues provides guidance for new endeavors that connect regional communities, and support young women. These independent efforts are especially important as Texas and the nation see the large and emerging Latino population greatly influencing future success.

CRADLE OF TEXAS ROAD, SUPPLEMENT FOUR

Sam Houston's Danville Speech, Editorial Comment

Two Commentaries extracted from *The Southern Intelligencer,*
Austin, Texas. Vol. 3, No. 7, Wednesday, October 6, 1858:

Commentary One, Editor of the Intelligencer

Montgomery County, Texas, September 15, 1858

Having heard General Houston at Danville, on the occasion of the Barbeque given him on the 11th inst., I have thought that a brief notice of his speech might be interesting to most of your readers. He commenced with a review of his course in the Senate at the last session, and said that he had sustained the leading measures of the administration, not alone because he approved them, but because in doing so, he felt that he was obeying the wishes of his constituents, who had so largely contributed to Mr. Buchanan's election.

He dwelt at some length upon his advocacy of a protectorate over Mexico, saying that it was peculiarly a southern measure, and one which, in view of the distracted and disorganized condition of that unhappy country, addressed itself to every consideration of sound policy and enlightened humanity—that it commended itself to the sagacity of the statesman, but timid and time-serving politicians were afraid of it, and had therefore defeated it; but eventually the wisdom of the measure would be recognized, and, like the annexation of Texas, it would be taken hold of by the masses and carried over the heads of politicians. That the encroachments of free-soil territory upon our borders, rendered the policy necessary to the integrity of our institutions, extending as it would, the area of slavery in a southern direction.

He spoke of the causes of his unpopularity in the South; and said they might all be traced to his unwavering adherence to and support of the Union of the States, which in a period, little more than three quarters of a century, had become the glory and the wonder of the world. He had opposed the passage of the Kanas bill, because it was not demanded by the exigencies of the times, nor asked for by any portion of the Southern people. Under the compromise measures of 1850, the country had enjoyed unexampled peace and prosperity; in the midst of which a demagogue from the North, for selfish and political purposes, introduced the Kansas bill, which he, Gen'l H. in his place in the Senate, denounced at the time as a firebrand, endangering the integrity of the Democratic party, detrimental to the interests of the South and the country. It was offered in the name of democracy, as a great boon to the South, but it was a transparent humbug. It was offered by that prince of humbugs, Stephen A. Douglas. The people, however, had awakened from their delusion upon the subject—the Kansas bill and its objects are now better understood, Douglas, at length, stood unmasked before the South, and throughout its wide borders there could be none found to do him reverence, "OH no, you never mention him

His name is never heard, Your lips are now forbid to speak That once familiar word."

But as the people of Kansas had organized a government, he, Gen'l. H. had voted for its admission, as the best means of getting the trouble out of the way, while Douglas had opposed its admission, and extremists North and South seemed to wish to keep the firebrand blazing.

He next passed in review, the causes of quarrel between the North and the South, and contended that nothing had yet transpired to justify a dissolution of the Union. The people of the North, so far, had confined themselves to voting, speaking, and publishing their views and sentiments, upon the subject of African Slavery; the exercise of these privileges were inalienable and guaranteed by the Constitution, and however much, sensible men might lament the course pursued by such fanatics in the North, as Abby Kelly, Garrison and Phillips, yet the evil was only augmented by the Abby Kelly's Garrisons and Phillips of the South, who foolishly joined in the quarrel, and hurled back epithet for epithet. That whenever the North should go so far as to lay the weight of its finger upon the rights of the South, the people of the South would unite as one man, to repel the insult and protect their rights, and there would be required no Southern League, in the language of Mr. Yankee, "to precipitate the Southern States into a revolution." He said he was wearied of hearing the senseless cant about "Southern Rights," as though the South had any rights not enjoyed in common with every section of the country. It had been the boast of our institutions, that they guarantied equal rights to every citizen and to every State. Then what rights had the South over the North, or the North over the South? Each sovereign State must be allowed to pass its own municipal laws, and to regulate its own domestic institutions, and to constitutionally change them whenever it chooses. He denounced the project of re-opening the African Salve trade. Its authors were dis-unionists, per se, and they sought to affect their object by widening the breach between the North and the South. He was equally severe upon the project of a Southern League, and said, its authors and objects were identical with those of the slave trade.

He ridiculed the remark recently made by Mr. Yankee, of Alabama, that the boys of this generation were wiser than the sages of the Revolution. Such sentiments, he regretted to say, were but too common. They furnished the best commentary upon the character of the times, and plainly indicated our tendency to anarchy, and revolution. As Mr. Yankee must have been an uncommonly bright youth, he wondered he had not when a boy, discovered the beauties of a Southern League. He said that his enemies had charged him with infidelity to the South! Though he had served his country in various capacities for more than forty years—though born and reared in the South; though his wife and children, his home and all his interest were in the South; and though more than one spot had been watered by his blood shed in defense of the South; yet all these had proved no shield against the injustice and absurdity of the charge. His enemies had ever been ready to seize upon and hold up to public condemnation, every act of his public life, that could possibly he tortured into an error, whilst his good acts were passed unnoticed. The Texan boundary embracing the vast territory for which we obtained from the United States ten millions of dollars, was first declared by him in a letter to Gen. Rusk; immediately after the battle of San Jacinto, which boundary, by his influence and during his first administration, became established by an act of the Congress of the Republic of Texas.

His remarks closed with a glowing eulogy upon the ladies, a large number being present. I have thus given you a hasty and I am satisfied a very imperfect sketch of a speech of more than two hours length, which thought was replete with much, that was inter-casting and eloquent. What is strange about Houston, is the fact that he speaks better now than he did ten years ago; **I heard a gentleman say, that he** had heard him fifty times; but had never heard him make a speech equal to that delivered at Danville.

Commentary Two, General Sam Houston at Danville

The [above] letter from a friend of Gen. Houston gives the same report of his speech which we have heard from several sources. Bating the implied effort of the General to defend his course upon the Kansas question, there are few who will not agree, that the sentiments are generally sound and patriotic and we trust that Gen. Houston has no enemy so bitter, as not to wish to see the veteran Texian battling stoutly for the cause of the South and the National Democracy.

The writer was the first, publicly to condemn Gen. Houston's speech upon Kansas. We stated then, as the highest authority and the public mind has since endorsed, that the argument about the Missouri restriction was fallacious, because Congress never had the power to pass the law; that the Indian treaties had abolished the restriction; and the Federal Government had thus carried slavery, upon the territories North of thirty-six thirty, and protected it there; that the separate nationality of the Indians was impossible; and therefore, the Indian sympathy was misspent; and that a Southern man should always distrust his own judgment, whenever he finds himself in the company of Black Republicans or Abolitionists— (Other Texas Congressmen will learn this fatal fact).

So because of these votes, and Gen Houston's sin of becoming a Know Nothing, and the advocate of the proscriptive principles and the "governmental organization" of that party, we opposed his election. But we allow the locus penetentae, and we give credit for the good deeds of all men. Rejecting the fallacious arguments of Douglas and Wise about an enabling act, and the manner of making a constitution, or applying for admission into the Union; and knowing that a State may be admitted as well without as with a constitution; and seeing that the Administration had staked so much upon the measure, we were glad to see him give the original and English bill his hearty support. We likewise felt that his disinterested support of the deficiency bill was kind. His opposition to the increase of the regular army, and his preference for volunteers, met our hearty concurrence.

At Washington, where there are no local resentments; and where all questions are regarded in a national point of view, we found that this support had enlisted for him the good feelings of the Administration, and of leading Democrats. And while we had no conversation with Gen. H. about his future course, we had hoped that when he came home, he would make a clean breast of it; declare for the Democracy as the only national party, able and willing to save the Union. Seeing the danger from extremists at both ends of the Union, we are willing to forgive much, to get national men of influence. We have had to forgive sinners almost as willful as Houston, and regret that we afterwards found some of them more proscriptive than they were when working shoulder to shoulder with "Old Sam in the Culvert." And now, if the Gen. is to "come back to the Democracy," (as approved ex. K. N. editors term it,) we protest against his bringing into our camps any more of the "usages" of the defunct party, or the planks of the Philadelphia platform. The politico-judicial-article-in-order-to-interpret-the-laws plank, is more than the Democracy can safely carry. But if the Gen. intends to bring along the further plank, that all laws are binding until the judges so selected, as a part of the political machine, declare the contrary, we will help to put up the bars which are now down, for the return of all stray sheep.

But we and be converted. The final perseverance of the saints is a good doctrine, when conjoined to good works and reformation: do not much fear the old Gen. upon these planks. We believe he was with President Jackson's views in the Georgia Missionary case. Repent, Gen. .

CRADLE OF TEXAS ROAD, SUPPLEMENT FIVE

Short Biography of Richard Williams

by Larry Foerster

Richard Williams was born in February 1808 in Milledgeville, Baldwin County, Georgia to the marriage of James Edward Williams and Nancy Hill. Williams arrived in Texas in 1834 as a single man from Georgia to presumably find his fortune in this new land.

It appears that after Richard Williams arrived in Texas in 1834 at the age of 26, he fought in several battles of the Texas Revolution, including the "Bexar campaign" in 1835 at the battle known as the "Grass Fight" where he was severely wounded by a canister shot while serving in Captain John M. Bradley's company. The shot struck a pistol at his side (thus his life was saved.) He remained nearby until the city of San Antonio was taken. His next term of service was in the campaign subsequent to the Battle of San Jacinto (April 21, 1836), after his marriage to Mary Miller in January 1836.

Richard Williams married Mary Miller on January 2, 1836 in Washington County (now Montgomery County), Texas. Mary Miller was the 3rd daughter of James Miller (who was born in Tennessee in 1792 and died in Texas in 1830) and Ruth ("Ruthie") Shannon, daughter of early Montgomery County settlers Owen Shannon and wife Margaret A. Montgomery Shannon, who lived northwest of what today is known as Dobbin.

It is reported that the Republic of Texas gave Richard Williams a large tract of land for his service in the War, and he and his wife Mary settled in Washington County east of what would become the Danville community. (Today the land is in northern Montgomery County along the Walker county line.) He built a cabin near the present site of the family cemetery, and he operated at various times a sawmill, gristmill, and cotton gin.

It appears that Richard Williams and his wife were settled on his land by late 1837, since he was one of several citizen land owners in what was then Washington County in October 1837 to petition the Republic of Texas for a new county with the Brazos River as the dividing line. The Act creating Montgomery County was passed on December 14, 1837.

The Tax Rolls of Montgomery County in 1838 (as compiled by Mary Peoples) shows that in June 1838 Richard Williams was listed as a property owner, but the rolls do not identify how many acres he owned.

Richard Williams and Mary Miller Williams reportedly had 13 children, only two of whom are known to be buried at the Richard Williams Cemetery: Leila Jacinto Williams (2nd child) died at age 3 on March 8, 1842, and Sam Houston Williams (3rd child) died reportedly in 1852. [NOTE: The Texas Historical Marker at the Cemetery identifies the Williams' as having only 10 children, that

Leila Jacinto Williams was the 3rd child, and that Sam Houston Williams died in 1852.]

In 1842, perhaps soon after the death of his young daughter Leila in March, then Captain Richard Williams lead a Montgomery County volunteer militia for the Somervell Expedition, organized by Alexander Somervell to invade Mexico at President Sam Houston's order. Along the way Williams became severely ill and left the force before it reached Mexico, thereby avoiding the fate of many of the men in the Expedition who were later captured and killed by the Mexican army. (One of the volunteers under Capt. Williams was William Henry Hulon, husband of Phoebe Reese Spillers, daughter of John and Frances Conger Spillers. Hulon was a farmer who raised his family of 7 children near the Danville community and later at age 46 joined the Danville Mounted Riflemen in May 1861.)

According to the Montgomery County Commissioners' Court Minutes in January 1845, the Court appointed Richard Williams, along with John Park, Jonathan H. Ridgeway, A.H. White, and Joseph Lindley, to mark and lay out a road commencing near Joseph Lindley's property, "running to Burches ferry on San Jacinto and make report of their actings and doings at the next term of this Court."

The Montgomery County Commissioners Court Minute Book indicates that Richard Williams was serving as Montgomery County Commissioner by 1849. According to the October 15, 1850 Federal census for Montgomery County, Richard Williams at age 42 owned property valued at $5000 (a significant sum for that time), was married to Mary (age 32) and had 7 living children ages 13 to 2 years. (Leila Jacinto had died in 1842).

In the 1872 Texas Almanac, Richard Williams was reported by J.H. Shepherd (himself one of the Montgomery County veterans of the Texas Revolution) to be "about 60 years old...looks as young as twenty-five years ago;" and at times suffered from his wound at the Grass Fight in 1835.

Richard Williams died on October 10, 1876 at age 68, and was buried on his property in the one-half acre family burial site alongside at least two of his children: Leila Jacinto Williams and Sam Houston Williams. His wife Mary Miller Williams died on November 9, 1894 and is buried next to her husband. A Part of the original Williams tract was purchased by Gene and Christina Molk in 1952 where they operated a family dairy farm for many years. The Williams burial site was largely neglected until about 1975 when the Montgomery County Historical Survey Committee fenced the site, and a Texas Historical Marker was placed at the cemetery.

There are reportedly 70 unmarked graves in the unfenced area of the cemetery and there is a separate fenced but neglected area where members of the Carroll family are buried, with markers dating back to the 1880's. Gene and Christina Molk, along with their daughter, are also buried in a separate section of the burial site, about 30 feet away from the Williams family tombstones. (These tombstones are in relatively good condition but desperately need to be cleaned.)

It is believed (but not yet confirmed) that the 1842 tombstone of Richard Williams' three-year old daughter, Leila Jacinto Williams, is the oldest known legible tombstone in Montgomery County.

The Richard Williams Cemetery is located about 6 miles east of Willis off of FM 1097 East. Turn left on the paved Bilnoski Road; drive about two miles to Molk Road, a paved county road; turn right and proceed down Molk Road until the county paving ends and then continue down the dirt road to the cemetery on the right. The gate is locked and Bart Molk, who lives in the house further down the drive, has the key. His brother Rick Molk can be contacted at 936-525-9218 or mayormolk@suddenlink.net .

Larry L. Foerster
April 22, 2012

INDEX

Royall, Richard 99
Rubio, Liz 188
Rummell, Marisa Olivares 116
Runnels, Hardin 58

S

Sabine River 12, 166, 167, 173
Saint Mary's Catholic Church 68
Salado, Hacienda 63
Salcedo, Manuel 12, 17, 156, 179, 180, 181
Salle, René Robert Cavelier Sieur de la Salle xiv, 43, 44, 45, 47, 51, 150, 151, 156, 157, 163, 164, 165, 166, 167, 168, 169, 170
Saltillo 6, 63
Sam Houston High School 142
Sam Houston Industrial and Training School 142
Sam Houston Normal Insitute 140, 143
Sam Houston School 142
Sam Houston State University v, 104, 140, 148, 156
San Antonio xv, 3, 5, 6, 11, 12, 13, 15, 16, 19, 21, 29, 30, 44, 46, 61, 62, 165, 166, 179, 180, 181, 182, 195
San Antonio Road 3, 5, 6, 11, 15, 19, 21, 46
San Diego 49
San Felipe 5, 6, 8, 58, 59
San Felipe, council of 5
San Jacinto 4, 5, 6, 14, 28, 31, 54, 57, 59, 60, 61, 62, 64, 72, 102, 103, 140, 167, 192, 196, 197
San Jacinto River 5, 6, 57
Santa Anna 30, 61, 72
Santisma Trinidad de Salcedo 11, 12, 14, 17, 156, 173, 180
Sawmill 109, 196
Sawmills 71, 109, 135, 196
Scarbrough, Maribel Garza 188
School 25, 105, 110, 112, 113, 114, 116, 119, 121, 124, 131, 133, 139, 140, 142, 143, 144, 188

Schreiber, Belle 131
Scott, Garret 38
Scott, Sir Walter 134
Scout Camp 111
Seamstresses 124
Second Republic of Texas 150, 152, 163, 166
Secretary of State 55, 99, 101, 180
Seguin 113
Senate 101, 189, 190
Senate Pro Tempore 58, 153
Senator 140
Service 36, 39, 48, 98, 99, 112, 113, 119, 195, 196
Settlement 5, 15, 16, 24, 29, 53
Shabaz, Ahia Dr. xvi, 127
Shaler, William 180
Shaman 19
Shannon, Aaron Colonel 102
Shannon, Jacob 68, 69
Shannon, Jacob Evergreen Cemetery 68, 69
Shannon, Margaret A. Montgomery 68, 69, 196
Shannon, Owen 68, 69, 196
Shannon, Ruth 196
Sharecropper 48
Shepherd, J. H. 197
Shiro 29, 30, 31, 150, 152, 153
Shootout, 1900 37, 38
Shot 63, 73, 109, 134, 153, 195
Shrine 13, 176, 177
Sindico Procurador 58
Slave 47, 131, 141, 142, 192
Slavery 191
Slaves 29, 112, 135, 145
Smith, Carl xvi
Smith, Henry 58, 99
Smith, Martha 59
Social xiv, 40, 48, 115, 116, 123, 125, 154, 174, 176
Sociology 126
Soil 14, 130

Union Baptist Association 102
Union Church 141
United States 11, 12, 13, 49, 55, 110,
111, 125, 130, 131, 132, 140, 144,
152, 163, 165, 166, 167, 168, 173,
174, 175, 178, 180, 184, 192
United States Mail 132
University v, 9, 23, 51, 104, 105, 110,
113, 126, 140, 142, 148, 155, 156,
157, 173, 188
University of Chicago 113
University of Houston 105, 126, 188
University of New Mexico 173
Upchurch, Denise 25
Upchurch, Robert 25
US Army Corps of Engineers 110
US-Mexican War 145, 168, 171
Utah 23, 168

V

Valladolid 177
Vatican 111
Velardo, Diana 188
Velasco 98, 167
Velasco, Battle of 98, 167
Vera Cruz 175
Veteran 64, 68, 134, 193
Vice President 35, 183
Viceroy 15, 16
Vick, Archie 120
Viesca, District of 6, 57, 60, 61
Village 28, 46, 54, 124, 133, 178
Virginia 30, 135, 142
Virgin, see Guadalupe or Mary 13, 50
Volunteer 116, 197

W

Wagon 103
Walker County 30, 144, 145, 148, 156
Walker, John G. 40
Walker, Robert J. 144
Walkers 144
Walker, Samuel H. 144

War 28, 37, 48, 59, 98, 100, 144, 145,
168, 171
Washington v, 3, 4, 7, 8, 9, 10, 24, 27,
35, 50, 53, 54, 56, 58, 59, 61, 69,
100, 142, 144, 150, 152, 156, 159,
160, 194, 196
Washington D. C. v, 142
Washington Municipality 3, 4, 7, 27, 54,
58, 69, 144, 150, 152
Washington-on-the-Brazos v, 3, 4, 7, 8,
9, 10, 24, 27, 35, 50, 53, 54, 56, 58,
59, 61, 69, 100, 142, 144, 150, 152,
156, 159, 160, 194, 196
Washington Town Company 54
Water 16
Watershed 6
Waverly 129, 133, 134, 135, 136, 137,
139, 150, 157
Waverly, New 135, 136, 137, 139, 150,
157
Waverly, Old 133, 135
Waverly Station 136
Weapon 28, 120
Weches 45
Wedding 36, 72
Wheelwright 141
Whitaker 27
Whitaker, Alex 27
White, A. H. 197
White Flag 63
White House Appointment 116
White Man's Union 38
Whites 124
Wife 12, 25, 28, 44, 48, 68, 69, 72, 102,
112, 121, 131, 144, 164, 192, 196,
198
Wilbarger 28, 33, 65, 160
Wilkerson, Wally Dr. 188
Wilkes County, Georgia 54
Willard, Jess 131
Williams, Mary Miller 196, 198
Williams, Richard Captain 134, 137,
156, 195, 196, 197, 198
Williams, Sam Houston 196, 198